INDEX

Preface	2
How to use this book	3

What — 5

What is Inclusive Design?	6
Timeline	10
Prejudices and preconceptions	12

Why — 15

Contexts are changing	16
How changing contexts affect your business	18
We can all be excluded	20
Article: The Business of Inclusive Design	22
Examples from business	28
Inclusive Design checklist	31

How — 33

People-centred design	34
Comparing approaches	38
The design process	39
Criteria tool	41
Eight Inclusive Design activities	42

Tools — 53

Research tools	54
Low contact:	
Questionnaire	56
Web forum	58
Natural observation	60
Medium contact:	
Interview	62
Research kit	64
Design provocation	66
High contact:	
Controlled observation	68
Workshop	70
Evaluation	72

Case studies — 75

Short case studies	
Power tools	76
Telecommunications	77
Homeware	78
Service	79
Automotive	80
Full case studies	
Transport	81
Packaging	84
Household products	86
Furniture	88
Service	90
Glossary	92
Further reading and references	94
Credits	95
Organisations and contributors	96

PREFACE

Are you searching for new competitive advantages?
Is your company operating in a market undergoing change?

Inclusive Design (termed Universal Design by the Norwegian government) is being written into legislation. Products and services will now have to meet these new criteria. This book shows how you can turn this challenge into opportunities for profitable innovation.

The Innovation for All programme, set up and run by the Norwegian Design Council, focuses precisely on this issue. It looks at how your company can develop better, more user-friendly products and services with little investment. Conducting research with people and involving them in your development process can give you new knowledge about your customers and lead you towards innovative solutions.

This publication is an introduction to Inclusive Design showing how it can be used as a strategy for better business. The idea is to inspire and motivate, demonstrating how industrial and commercial enterprises can benefit from a people-centred approach to design and development. This book aims to be a practical guide and manual that contains the basic information you need to understand Inclusive Design and begin practising it.

It is aimed at business leaders, managers, marketers and designers who are involved in design, development, research or specification. It explains the Inclusive Design process, making the case for using it both commercially and creatively. It also provides a practical guide to techniques for applying it.

The content has been compiled by individuals who have had extensive, practical experience in working with Inclusive Design in a business context. The book shares insights and learnings gathered over the years and is presented in an 'easy-to-access' format.

Case studies and examples explain how companies from across the globe have benefited from Inclusive Design. A practice-based section details nine research techniques for engaging with people and bringing their points of view into the design process. Throughout the pages there are images, insights, quotes and tips for you to use.

Onny Eikhaug
Onny Eikhaug
Innovation for All Programme
Norwegian Design Council

HOW TO USE THIS BOOK

There are five main sections to the book each marked by a different colour.

WHAT	*Describes what Inclusive Design is and gives a brief history*
WHY	*Tells you why you should use Inclusive Design and outlines benefits*
HOW	*Demonstrates how to use Inclusive Design in your existing processes*
TOOLS	*Step-by-step guidance for conducting research with people*
CASE STUDIES	*Examples of how companies have used Inclusive Design*

The book contains various types of information for you to use in different ways. It presents practical and accessible advice. Key elements in each section include:

- **Text** to give detailed insight into topics
- **Images** to bring content to life
- **Illustrations** to represent ideas visually
- **Quotes** for you to repeat to other people
- **Bullet points** to present advice clearly
- **Fact boxes** to summarise key information
- **Case studies** showing business examples

WHAT

This section gives an introduction to Inclusive Design. It presents the practice, describes the potential and provides a brief history. A definition of Inclusive Design and related terms are outlined and prejudices and preconceptions are addressed. A timeline of some important events shows how the concept has evolved globally.

WHAT IS INCLUSIVE DESIGN?

Inclusive Design is an approach to design and a business strategy. It aims to design mainstream products, services and environments that are accessible and attractive to the largest possible number of people.

Inclusive Design involves people within the design or development process, using a variety of research techniques to understand their needs and uncover their aspirations. By addressing individuals with differences in ability, age, gender and culture, it can lead to more varied and inspirational consumer insight. Importantly, it can also be applied when developing any type of design.

Design can be simply described as a process of examining a problem and creating a solution. Inclusive Design brings the perspective of real people to that problem, inspiring a multitude of viewpoints and unexpected ideas. The resulting solutions can therefore be more varied, innovative and user-friendly, bringing new thinking to familiar challenges within your business.

Inclusive Design is set to become an important design movement in the 21st century, building on the increasing interest in it and social advancements of the last century. Involving end users within the design and development process is becoming a more successful and proven way of engaging with consumers, and one that is also driven by legislation.

WHERE DID IT COME FROM?
Historically Inclusive Design focused on older or disabled people who were generally excluded by mainstream design. However, its people-centred techniques can be used to address other marginalised groups within society. More importantly, these methods are now being seen as a business strategy, opening a direct route to consumer-led innovation.

Those communities that are traditionally ignored by designers and businesses can provide the strongest inspiration for ideas that are also applicable to mainstream markets. For example, packaging that is developed for people with arthritis can be easier to open for us all. An automatic door benefits everyone, not just older and disabled people.

"Design for the young and you exclude the old; design for the old and you include the young"

Bernard Isaacs, Founding Director, Birmingham Centre for Applied Gerontology

INCLUSIVE DESIGN IS NOT JUST ABOUT GOOD INTENTIONS – IT IS ALSO ABOUT GOOD BUSINESS

Above, left and opposite page: We can all experience barriers such as stairs or heavy doors. Inclusive Design solutions can benefit everyone. Automatic doors, lever taps and spacious private bathrooms with wall-hung toilets make daily living easier

INCLUSIVE DESIGN HIGH-RETURN WAY NEW IDEAS

WHY IT IS RELEVANT TO YOU

It is becoming increasingly difficult to understand the complexity of today's consumers. Inclusive Design can help a company define and implement more meaningful ways to engage with people that will enable deeper understanding of a particular market sector and what they might demand from your product or service.

Design is also being recognised as a strategic tool for innovation rather than just being used to address aesthetics. Inclusive Design can enable design to have a more effective role in any development process. Instead of just talking to people to validate ideas at the end of a project, users can play a lead role in defining issues and helping to set direction. User involvement can be beneficial at all stages of a project.

Conducting research with people is essential and can help influence design criteria alongside factors such as cost, materials, safety, technology and sustainability. Consumer relevance is equally important to any of these. Inclusive Design techniques can be added to existing working practice within a company at little cost, but will give a high return on investment through the benefits it brings.

The concept of an 'average person' is holding less and less credibility. With the rapid exchange of information and ideas, our social and cultural definitions are constantly changing and people cannot easily be categorised into neat groups. Whilst traditional market segmentation allows companies to target and focus by generalising consumer types, Inclusive Design can offer ways of qualitatively describing individual customers, bringing marketing data to life. This approach goes beyond describing physical needs to helping you understand the desires and aspirations of people in your potential market.

WHY YOU SHOULD BE INTERESTED

As an approach, Inclusive Design holds many benefits for businesses and designers. For designers, it is a source of inspiration and an opportunity for innovation. It can uncover problems or issues that have not previously been addressed. For businesses the resulting products, services and environments can widen the consumer base, increase appeal and improve competitiveness. By adopting an Inclusive Design process, companies will also be better placed to comply with current and future legislation.

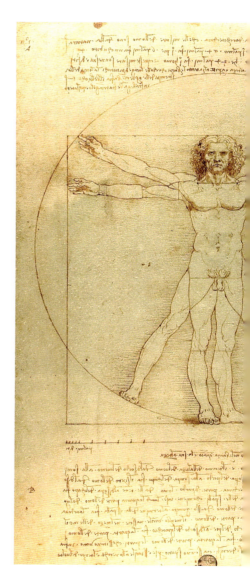

Above: The Vitruvian Man by Leonardo Da Vinci captures idealised, average proportions. Inclusive Design recognises our differences

S A LOW-COST, TO GENERATE

DEFINITIONS
Inclusive Design is sometimes used interchangeably with two other terms, Universal Design and Design for All. All three have a similar purpose but have different origins and are used in various parts of the world.

INCLUSIVE DESIGN
Defined in 2000 by the UK Government as "products, services and environments that include the needs of the widest number of consumers". It has a history stretching back to the social ideals in Europe that materialised after World War II. These include healthcare and housing for everyone. Inclusive Design is used within Europe and goes beyond older and disabled people to focus on other excluded groups to deliver mainstream solutions.

UNIVERSAL DESIGN
This term originated in the USA and is now adopted by Japan and the Pacific Rim. It started with a strong focus on disability and the built environment. Driven by the large number of disabled Vietnam War veterans, it was modelled on the Civil Rights Movement that promised "full and equal enjoyment … of goods and services". It has been a driving force in establishing American legislation regarding older and disabled people.

DESIGN FOR ALL
Closely related to Inclusive Design, Design for All started by looking at barrier-free accessibility for people with disabilities but has become a strategy for mainstream, inclusive solutions. As highlighted by the European Commission, it is about ensuring that environments, products, services and interfaces work for people of all ages and abilities in different situations and under various circumstances. This term is used in continental Europe and Scandinavia.

There are other terms that are sometimes used with varying relevance to Inclusive Design. A few include Co-design, People-centred Design, User-focused Design and Trans-generational Design. Please see the Glossary for further information.

European milestones

1960 (Italy)
First Paralympics established in Rome

1963 (Norway)
Norwegian Design Council founded to promote design to industry

1963 (UK)
Architect Selwyn Goldsmith creates building guidelines for wheelchair users

1968 (Denmark)
Susanne Koefoed Creates the International Symbol of Access

ERGONOMIDESIGN

1979 (Sweden)
User-centred Ergonomi Design Gruppen established

1948 (UK)
Ludwig Guttmann organises wheelchair athletics for war veterans

1948 — **Global milestones** — 1976

1954 (USA)
Supreme Court establishes that "Separate is not equal"

1964 (USA)
The Civil Rights Act signed. A blueprint for future laws

1979 (UN)
UN Convention on the Elimination of All Forms of Discrimination against Women

1976 (UN)
United Nations international year for disabled persons

A BRIEF HISTORY

A selection of key events in the development of Inclusive Design from a European and global perspective.

1998 (EU)
The Ford Focus is developed with older drivers in mind

2000 (UK)
The UK government defines Inclusive Design

2005 (Norway)
The Innovation for All programme started at Norwegian Design Council

2010 (EU)
The European Commission working on an EU Disability Strategy for 2010-2020

1999 (UK)
The Helen Hamlyn Centre is founded focusing on Inclusive Design

2004 (Norway)
The launch of the first Government Plan of Action for Universal Design 2004-2008

2009 (Norway)
The Anti-discrimination and Accessibility Act came into effect

1991 (Norway)
Norwegian State Council on Disability created

1991   2010

1986 (USA)
Apple Computer builds easy access into their operating system

1990 USA)
Oxo International introduces its Good Grips kitchen utensils

1998 (Canada)
First Canadian National Symposium on Disability Studies

2006 (UN)
UN Convention on the Rights of Persons with Disabilities

1985 (USA)
Universal Design was defined by architect Ron Mace

1990 (USA)
Americans with Disabilities Act passed

1997 (USA)
Seven principles of Universal Design created

1992 (Japan)
First International Conference for Universal Design

2003 (Japan)
International Association for Universal Design inaugurated

PREJUDICES & PRECONCEPTIONS

INCLUSIVE DESIGN IS...

1. When built into the design process, Inclusive Design can actually improve profit, add value and increase market appeal. Conducting research with people does not cost much but what can be expensive are recalls, retrofitting and unpopular design that does not sell.

2. Inclusive Design actually leads to innovation. Companies such as Toyota, BT (UK Tele-communication company) and Panasonic have all been recognised with Inclusive Design awards for exciting, mainstream designs.

3. Inclusive Design can be applied to any branch of design or market sector including services, environments, interfaces, packaging and graphics. Websites, electronic menus, software, signage, and wayfinding are also examples of non-physical applications of Inclusive Design.

4. People can face exclusion in many other ways including social, economic, cognitive, physical, by age or gender. Inclusive Design goes beyond accessibility and disability to address this wider range of issues. It can be applied to improve most mainstream products and services.

5. Inclusive Design is not about 'special needs' design or specialised equipment. It is design for the widest possible range of users. A stair lift only helps those in wheelchairs, whereas an elevator is accessible to everyone and does not discriminate according to ability.

There are many prejudices and preconceptions about Inclusive Design. These are due to lack of understanding or oversimplification. These pages reveal and counter some of the most common ones.

6. ...NOT FOR ME

7. ...NOT CONCERNED WITH AESTHETICS

8. ...FOR NICHE MARKETS SUCH AS OLDER PEOPLE

9. ...JUST ANOTHER BUZZWORD

10. ...ONLY ABOUT PUBLIC SERVICES

6. Everyone can benefit from Inclusive Design including you. For example, most of us can have some form of disability whether dyslexia, short sightedness, allergies or a broken leg. Inclusive Design can make packaging easier to open, signs easier to read, and services easier to use.

7. Aesthetics play a major role in the acceptance and comprehension of a design and should always be considered. Many companies create designs using Inclusive Design principles that have given them an edge. Attractive design and Inclusive Design are not mutually exclusive.

8. Inclusive Design can be used to open up new market segments. Talking to real people can uncover consumer needs that have not been articulated before, putting you ahead of competitors. What might be considered the niche market today could be the market of tomorrow.

9. Inclusive Design has a history and a future. It is now being written into legislation and companies that ignore this could be liable. Far from being a trend, Inclusive Design can be considered a design movement, and one that will be increasingly important this century.

10. Public services are just one obvious application, but Inclusive Design equally applies to any commercial design that is used by a large number of people. Examples include mobile phones, websites, packaging, retail environments and transport to name a few.

WHY

This section explains why you should engage with Inclusive Design. It contains an article that makes the case for designers and for business, showing how this can lead to innovation, profit and increased market share. It outlines changes taking place in the world and gives examples of major companies that have benefited from an inclusive approach.

CONTEXTS ARE CHANGING

Design has to respond to changes that are taking place in the world around us. The diagram below outlines some examples, looking at selected issues from a global to individual perspective.

As of January 2010 US President Barack Obama had 7,128,277 Facebook fans

Every second, 310 kg of toxic chemicals are released into our air, land, and water by industrial facilities around the world

In Western Europe, 80% of car journeys are below 60km, and 20% of cars never go any further

There are 749 vehicles per 1,000 people in the mature markets of the G7 countries

**ENVIRONMENT
DEVELOPING COUNTRIES**

**TRAVEL
PUBLIC OPINION
SOCIETY**

During 2010 China will become the world's largest consumer of energy and the second-largest car market

In 2007, 50% of the world's population was living in cities or towns. This will increase to 70% by 2050

In Norway 1 in 10 people are immigrants or born to parents who are immigrants

3 out of 10 Norwegians say they have health issues that affect their daily life

A quarter of the Norwegian population uses over three prescriptions every day

Globally, there are more than 1 billion overweight adults. 300 million are clinically obese

Google is visited by 77 percent of the worldwide internet audience

Norwegians over 45 hold more than 70% of the population's wealth

Those over 55 have more than NOK 300 billion to spend each year

314 million people worldwide are visually impaired – a population size that would rank 4th after China, India and the US

For every person entering the labour market in Scandinavia, three will retire. This ratio will double by 2017

In Norway, both women and men spend around six hours a day on leisure activities

Women make more than 80% of purchasing decisions but 83% of the creative industry are men

In the 10 newest EU member states 1 in 4 people have some form of disability

SERVICE DESIGN
HEALTHCARE
INTERNET

LEISURE
WORKING LIVES
SPENDING POWER
HOUSEHOLD
COMMUNICATION

ABILITY
GENDER
AGEING

3 million Norwegians in a population of 4.8 million go online every week

In Europe internet purchases increased by 110% between 2004 and 2008

In 2008 there were 4,017,249,000 mobile phones in the world

850 000 people live alone in Norway. 30% live in Oslo

By 2020 half of European adults will be aged 50 or over

10% of the world's population is 60 or older. In 2050 the number is estimated to increase by 100%

HOW CHANGING CONTEXTS AFFECT YOUR BUSINESS

The graphic on the previous pages illustrates how social contexts are changing and highlights relevant factors and trends. The themes outlined here detail some important market challenges that Inclusive Design can help to address. The opportunities are significant.

THEME 1. **EMBRACING DIVERSITY**

Factors: emerging markets, ignored markets and diverse populations
Effect: wider appeal for products and services

Design and businesses will have to be sensitive to more diverse markets if they are to maintain or expand their appeal. Emerging markets are beginning to become powerful consumer bases in their own right.

The growth in immigrant populations in Europe implies that businesses need to be aware of cultural diversity when designing new products, services or environments.

Diversity should also include gender equality and differences in ability and age. Inclusive Design can help you to understand and embrace diversity and find ways to appeal to a wider market.

THEME 2. **CONSUMERS ARE NOT STEREOTYPES**

Factors: global stereotyping, multi-layered personas, complexity of individuals
Effect: market segmentation, individual appeal, challenging preconceptions

People no longer fall into traditionally defined market categories. New typologies are constantly being created and people can often display multiple and changeable characteristics depending on context. People can no longer be defined by factors such as gender, age, disability or cultural background – lifestyle, value, attitudes and personal ethics all play a role.

Market segmentation has to use qualitative as well as quantitative measures to address human complexity. Designing for people must take a more sophisticated approach and not just cater for mainstream stereotypes.

Inclusive Design can help to overcome preconceptions and assumptions about target groups and expand our understanding of the consumer psyche.

THEME 3. LIFESTYLES ARE CHANGING

Factors: technology, medicine, urbanisation, social structure, consumer lifestyle
Effect: new contexts of use, new markets give new opportunities

Technology is a main driver in changing the way people live, work and communicate and this has influenced the structure and behaviour of individuals in society. Improved medicine is leading to longer, healthier lives with greater burden on social models of healthcare. Rapid urbanisation is creating large cities that struggle under congestion with increasing demand for services and supplies.

Family structures are changing with people spread over greater distances and up to four generations still alive in a family. Single living is on the rise as the numbers of newly-divorced or widowed people increase. Businesses will need to understand the changing lifestyles of their customers and the different contexts that they are now operating in.

THEME 4. VALUE STRUCTURES ARE CHANGING

Factors: changing values and aspirations
Effect: mapping trends, strengthening brand value

What people desire and value is changing. Several key value drivers for design currently include simplicity, efficiency, user-friendliness, sustainability and ethically sound design.

Inclusive Design allows you to map these changes and keep up to date with peoples' aspirations and expectations.

Improved awareness will help to design desirable products and improve brand image perception. It can also allow companies to 'future-map' activities and respond to societal trends as they happen.

WE CAN ALL BE EXCLUDED

Design generally caters for the mainstream user. They are typically young, able-bodied, right-handed, male, technology literate, have money and belong to the majority race and culture.

But who do you know who fits this description? Is it all of the people you know, some of them or only a few?

This ideal consumer is a minority and is not representative of the wider population. Most people are typically excluded in one or more ways.

All of us fall outside of the mainstream at some point in our lives and as a result, we can find the designed world around us more difficult.

There are many forms of exclusion. A few are given to the right as examples but the list is not exhaustive.

AGE
Older people are routinely ignored as consumers or as active members of the economy yet they are a majority market. We are all ageing and living longer. Other age groups can also be excluded when categorising consumers. A target group of 18-35 year olds excludes most of society.

ABILITY
Disability is not limited to wheelchair users and many conditions such as diabetes can be less obvious. We all have some disability whether minor or major, permanent or temporary. These can be sensory, physical or cognitive. Even a minor condition such as an allergy can be disabling.

GENDER
Women are underserved as consumers yet are key decision makers for most household purchases. Many products and services do not include women, representing missed opportunities across the globe. Increased participation of women at all levels in society will bring about change.

RACE
Immigration and migration has increased the ethnic and cultural flow into most major cities. However, lack of integration and ghettoisation prevents some communities from being included in mainstream society. The result is evident in education, employment, politics and economics.

FINANCE
Many people across the world struggle at the minimum level of subsistence. In developed countries this translates into lack of healthcare, housing or education. In developing countries, this can mean living on less than $1 a day. The same design often has to work in both settings.

GEOGRAPHY
Even within a country or city, different areas can have varying standards of healthcare, life expectancy, services and utilities. At a global level, populations in some countries can be further excluded. Geography can dictate access to energy, clean water, staple food and natural resources.

The bulls-eye diagram represents the total potential market that you could appeal to and includes a variety of people across it.

Source: Jeremy Myerson, RCA Helen Hamlyn Centre

Most companies only focus on a target customer who is typically younger, average and mainstream. This means your market will only fill the first few rings on the bulls-eye excluding everyone who is outside of this focus.

Looking at people who are generally excluded can only broaden your focus and increase the market potential for a design. These are shown here by the figures in the outer rings of the bulls-eye or placed outside of it.

THE BUSINESS OF INCLUSIVE DESIGN

This article is a position piece that details how Inclusive Design can improve business strategy. It draws together the ideas from across the publication into one text.

A GROWING IMPORTANCE

One of the challenges facing the global business community is to have a wider perspective when engaging with design. It is no longer a question of using design to meet purely aesthetic, functional or emotional needs. Design can also play an essential role in promoting sustainability, enabling human rights and creating social inclusion.

Companies that can concentrate their innovation process around understanding real consumers, respond to emerging trends and then meet these challenges using design can increase profitability and leave the competition behind.

As well as describing an approach, Inclusive Design is most effective when put into practice. It allows companies to view existing customers in a new way and to expand into previously untapped markets.

Since Inclusive Design promotes design for human diversity, social inclusion and equality, it has great resonance in the current political climate where addressing human rights and exclusion is high on the agenda.

Inclusive Design strategies can help companies to be more socially responsible by enabling greater diversity in the workforce, providing equal opportunities for employees and by active participation in the social arena. This can form a key part of a company's Corporate Social Responsibility and elevate its public perception.

Above: Recognising diversity, addressing social inclusion and designing for human aspiration are all becoming increasingly important

NEW LEGISLATION – NEW OPPORTUNITIES

Both nationally and internationally, governments and policymakers are writing Inclusive Design into new laws and standards. Legislation is being passed in order to counter discrimination and minimise exclusion. The United Nations, the European Council, the European Union and the Nordic Council of Ministers have all introduced directives regarding the principles of Inclusive Design.

In 2006 the United Nations agreed on the Convention on the Rights of Persons with Disabilities. This was the first human rights treaty of the 21st century, aimed at increasing and upholding the rights of the estimated 650 million disabled people across the world. In Norway, the Public Procurement Act stipulates that public procurers are required to choose product and service solutions that meet Inclusive Design criteria. Suppliers who comply with these demands will be preferred.

FACT

By 2012, close to half the adult population of Norway will be aged over 50

"If a company is prepared to spend 3 per cent of its turnover on technology, it might achieve the same effect through design with only 0.3 per cent"

Krister Ahlström, Design Matters

The scope of new legislation has a far-reaching effect. For example, all new public buildings, environments and services in Norway will have to fulfil the requirements of Inclusive Design as per new legislation. Public transport and public electronic communication services will also have to be accessible to people with different needs and abilities (see page 94-95 for links).

However, whilst new legislation can be seen as a challenge, companies who adopt an Inclusive Design approach can turn this into an opportunity and even a competitive advantage. Aligning business practice with changes in law and policy means that you will become the preferred option in the future. For example, in Norway, the hotel star-rating system has specific Inclusive Design requirements for accessibility and service for all guests. Hotels that meet these requirements can get a higher rating and increase their market profile.

Above: This Norwegian low-entrance bus and bus station meets the EU's new transport directives. The system is one of Europe's most inclusive designs and is in daily use in Drammen

A people-centred design process is not only a strategy to solve problems but a potent strategy for identifying problems to solve.

A CREATIVE STRATEGY

Designers in particular have a role in demonstrating and selling the value of Inclusive Design to their clients, managers and business colleagues. The close relationship between designers and the development process means that they are ideally placed to incubate an Inclusive Design approach or champion it within an organisation. Those designers who have built up expertise and experience in Inclusive Design can differentiate themselves from their peers and be more attractive in today's competitive markets.

The dichotomy between meeting user needs and working within commercial constraints can provide a space in which designers are pushed to innovate and create inventive solutions that satisfy both demands. The point of overlap between 'commercial interests' and 'social interests' in any project represents the greatest potential for innovation (see diagram below).

INCREASING MARKET POTENTIAL

Inclusive Design can help to increase market potential by widening the appeal of a design beyond the primary target market. At the same time it maintains the attraction for customers within the primary segment, simply because the solution is better for everyone.

The pyramid diagram on the facing page demonstrates this potential for expansion. There are four market segments as described. At the bottom is the main market, or primary segment characterised by healthy, able-bodied customers often called the average consumer.

The next segment represents a large number of people, those who need some individual adjustment to live in the designed world. For example, these could include those wearing glasses, left-handed individuals, people with dyslexia, expectant mothers, travellers with heavy luggage, low vision or hearing impaired groups. This area holds the biggest potential for companies to address as shown by the expanding purple area in the diagram.

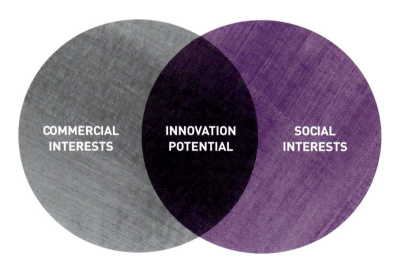

PEOPLE-CENTRED STRATEGY FOR PROFITABLE INNOVATION

FACT

In a UK survey, 85% of people reported frustrations and difficulties in setting up and using a new mobile phone

The top two segments show people who need specialised design, assistive technology or personal assistance to complete simple daily activities such as bathing, eating or drinking. Since their needs differ greatly from the mainstream, they are generally not considered to be primary markets for an Inclusive Design approach.

Consumers, especially the marginalised groups in the individual adjustment segment, represent a powerful tool for innovation giving companies a way of exploring needs that current designs have not yet addressed.

A HOLISTIC WAY OF THINKING

An Inclusive Design strategy does not need to be limited to the design process. It can be a foundation for companies to base their entire business philosophy on.
An inclusive way of thinking can impact on employment policy, personnel management, customer service, communications strategy and marketing for example.

This implies that the design department and other areas of the organisation must cooperate in formulating a holistic approach that roots itself in company culture, policy and practice. Implementation at both management level and throughout the organisation is equally important.

Practising Inclusive Design and conducting people-centred research requires a minimum amount of investment when compared to technological research and product development. This can therefore offer a low-tech, cost-saving and uncomplicated method for innovation with low barriers for implementation in both the short term and long term. It is also suitable for both small, medium and large companies and can yield immediate results.

EXPAND THE MARKET POTENTIAL
Ref. Knut Nordby 2003

CAN YOUR COMPANY AFFORD TO IGNORE THEM?

THE AFFLUENT OLDER CONSUMER
Although there are many groups who are excluded by mainstream design, one of the most important (and rewarding) to design for, are older people.

Older people make up the fastest growing market segment and possess substantial purchasing power. In 2012, around half of Norway's adult population will be aged 50 or over. By 2050 the number of people over the age of 67 will have doubled.

It is a myth that seniors are low spenders. In reality, the 'silver shopper' represents one third of the population and holds 75% of total private assets. Given their record-breaking purchasing power and their willingness to spend, older consumers are fast becoming the most powerful consumer group. They account for the most spending on health, well-being, travel and luxury goods in Norway, something that is reflected in other countries across the globe.

They are an opinionated, demanding and diverse consumer group who are comfortable with consumerism but have yet to be fully included by mainstream design.

They are generally not recognised as the 'real spenders' by industry. They receive very little attention from marketing and designers rarely accommodate their needs. In Scandinavia, women aged 55-65 spend the most on clothing yet relatively few companies address them.

LIFESTAGES AND ECONOMY

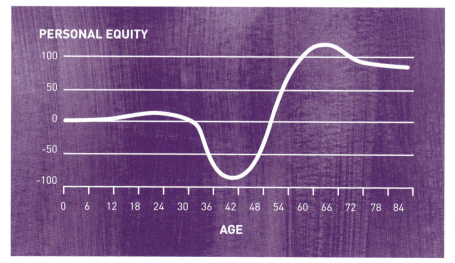

Left: Personal equity such as income and assets only start to exceed expenditure at age 45 as shown by the sharp upturn in the graph

FACT

Every third krone paid out in salaries goes to someone aged over 55. In total, this group has more than NOK 300 billion to spend each year and this figure is growing all the time

Above: UK retailer Marks & Spencer increased sales to the over 50's by employing Twiggy as a model. 'Trendy' was not defined as 'young'

"A young man will never buy an old man's car and neither will an old man buy an old man's car"

Alesandro Coda, Co-ordinator, Fiat Autonomy Project

As we grow older, our sight, hearing, muscle strength, motor skills and cognitive powers will reduce as natural part of the ageing process. Designers should therefore place an emphasis on functionality, user-friendliness and simplicity without compromising for aesthetics or desirability.

A new trend is emerging amongst older consumers, especially those aged between 60 and 70. They are remortgaging their homes in order to maintain or increase their standard of living. Some Norwegian banks have successfully reacted to this opportunity, creating new, tailor-made financial products and services to support this. These assets are now being channelled into higher levels of consumption meaning that market sectors other than banks could respond to this age group's demands in a similar way.

For people aged 75 and over, enabling them to live longer in their own homes by designing more inclusive and accessible domestic environments as well as services can save a significant amount of money and improve quality of life. Fewer will need care facilities and draw on already overburdened healthcare systems.

EXAMPLES FROM BUSINESS

Companies and organisations from around the world are using Inclusive Design to improve their offer to customers. Six case studies drawn from different industries are outlined below. They point to a different way of thinking and have met with success.

PUBLISHING
Rolling Stone magazine

Only 12 per cent of visually impaired people in the US can read Braille, a tactile language for non-sighted communication. The challenge taken up by Sean Donahue from Los Angeles based consultancy ResearchCenteredDesign, was to reinterpret a magazine in a more creative way for people with visual impairments that also brought benefit for fully sighted people.

Rolling Stone magazine was chosen as a focus and the result was a hybrid publication that combined different forms of communication. Text, Braille, tactile elements and graphics form a magazine where touch plays as important a role as reading. Images are raised from the page allowing readers to feel the form of a singer's face or single out Braille elements that double as artwork.

All the important elements of a magazine were reinterpreted to allow readers to use senses other than sight and provide new ways of addressing the 15 million people with visual impairment in the US. Publishers were quickly persuaded of the approach as the magazine was distributed and met with positive response from fully sighted and visually impaired people alike.

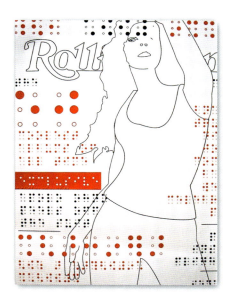

SERVICE
www.government.no

The Norwegian government's award-winning website has been highly rated in recent quality assessments carried out by the Agency for Public Management and eGovernment. The aim was to focus on creating 'an information society for all' and to measure the accessibility of public sites.

The site was highly rated for being user-oriented in expression, content, structure and navigation as well as taking advantage of the opportunities provided by web technology.

The jury commended the themed structure of the website and the fact that it is in both Norwegian dialects. One section posts public hearings helping to contribute to more open government and enabling broader dialogue with citizens. The site has maintained a high level of quality over time and is one of the few that has large documents in HTML format.

The Norwegian government has created this official website in line with the Accessibility and Anti-discrimination Law effective from 1 January 2009. This law will apply to all new public websites by July 2011 and existing websites must be adjusted to meet the requirements in the future.

HOME APPLIANCE
Panasonic washing machine

Japan has one of the most rapidly ageing populations and has an established focus on Inclusive Design, realising the commercial potential.

Leading Japanese companies formed the International Association for Universal Design in 2003 (Universal Design is the Japanese term for Inclusive Design). This organisation now has 144 members, including household names and global brands such as Panasonic, Mitsubishi and Toyota. The tilted-drum washing machine from Panasonic is good example of how Inclusive Design thinking can create product differentiation in a highly competitive market. Panasonic developed their new, energy efficient washing machine with an angled door placed in a more accessible position. People do not need to bend over to load, unload or see inside the machine.

The result was better for a wider range of customers and has a unique selling point: easier handling of kilos of laundry. The angled door, illuminated and tilted drum and programmable controls make the machine easier to use.

SPORTS EQUIPMENT
Swix Nordic walking poles

Sticks have long been used to assist walking but recently a new type of product, the trekking pole, has emerged. Whereas the walking stick is considered to be an aid for elderly people, the trekking pole is regarded as a sport product.

Nordic walking poles can improve fitness for all ages and fitness levels, appealing to anyone from cross-country athletes to those simply looking to exercise. Nordic walking can provide a 40% more effective workout than a regular walk as it activates additional muscle groups in the upper body. Older people can enjoy the benefits of better posture and balance whilst reducing shock loading to the knees, hips and back.

Trekking poles are a good example of inclusive, mainstream design as the product appeals to a broad user group. In 2004 there were more than 3.5 million Nordic walkers in Europe with interest growing across the globe. Swix has developed Nordic walking trekking poles since 2000 focusing on the sports and leisure market. Sales are steadily increasing with annual figures reaching more than 100,000 poles.

> *"Mature and elderly drivers are becoming an increasingly large percentage of the motoring public. So, with the Third Age Suit, we believe we have an advantage in knowing what that large demographic group demands"*
>
> Richard Perry-Jones, Vice President for Product Development, Ford

AUTOMOTIVE
Ford Focus

The Focus is a small family car that meets Ford of Europe's aim of creating a 'world car', a vehicle that could be sold across the globe. The Focus has been a runaway success from its European launch in 1998 to the current model in production. It was the best-selling car in the world between 1999 and 2004.

The Focus' designers and engineers went through workshops to understand the effects of ageing and the needs of the growing numbers of older drivers. A 'Third Age Suit' – that simulates the reduction in functional abilities, vision, dexterity, range of motion and strength that all occur with age – was used by the team to ensure that the requirements of older customers were met. For example, difficulties in accessing the vehicle led to bigger door openings and reduction in vision was addressed by using large, high contrast dials and switches.

Importantly, the Focus was never marketed as an older person's car

as the design improvements benefited everyone. It has won over 60 awards including 13 Car of the Year awards. UK motoring magazine Autocar named it the 'best family car ever' in 2003.

PRODUCT DESIGN
SAS coffee pot

Industrial designer Maria Benktzon and Ergonomidesign colleague Sven-Eric Juhlin developed a new, ergonomically improved coffee pot for SAS Airlines between 1984-1987. The old pot was made of stainless steel and weighed 2.5 kilogrammes when full. Many of the cabin crew developed strain injuries as a result.

On the old pot the handle was placed far from the centre of gravity which meant that the pot's weight put serious strain on the arm and wrist. The goal was to reduce the distance between the wrist and the centre of gravity of the liquid. The new pot also had to be drip-proof, fit into storage boxes, withstand major temperature changes and survive rough handling.

The SAS coffee pot places the handle almost over the main compartment reducing the strength needed to hold the pot. In this way the design addresses the needs of airline cabin crews by balancing the weight. It also proves ergonomically beneficial for everyone with weaker hands.

The coffee pot is still in use on over 30 airlines, and over 300,000 pots have been produced so far by Norplast in Norway.

CHECKLIST

Can I apply 'Inclusive Design' to my project?

Inclusive Design principles can always be applied when developing any product, environment or service. Below is a checklist to help you to decide why Inclusive Design should be applied.

Please note: the word 'product' is used in the questions below. This could be substituted for design, service, environment etc.

MARKET
- [ ] Can you think of a person for whom your product would be challenging to use?
- [ ] Are people with a range of ages and abilities going to use your product?
- [ ] Do members of the public interact with your product?
- [ ] Could your product appeal to a wider market?
- [ ] Could your product be more relevant to its target group?
- [ ] Could your product be used beyond its target group?
- [ ] Do you think the needs of your target market are changing?

COMPETITORS
- [ ] Are you operating in a mature market?
- [ ] Do you wish to develop new competitive advantages?
- [ ] Could increased user-friendliness give you a competitive edge?
- [ ] Is your aim to innovate rather than imitate?
- [ ] Is customer satisfaction important to the success of your product?
- [ ] Is public perception important to your company?

PRODUCT
- [ ] Could your product be more intuitive?
- [ ] Are your customers dissatisfied with any aspect of your product?
- [ ] Do you think that having better information about your users would improve your product?
- [ ] Is the usability of your product important?
- [ ] Could your product be better presented to your customers?
- [ ] Are you looking for new product ideas?

RESOURCES
- [ ] Do you wish to base your design decisions on real-world evidence?
- [ ] Do you want to know what the key issues are facing your customers?
- [ ] Do you want to know how your product could be improved?
- [ ] Could understanding the limitations or successes of your product be useful in the future development?

If you answered yes to five or more of these questions then an Inclusive Design approach will add value to your process. On the following pages, you will find a description of practical approaches and methods to help you implement Inclusive Design.

HOW

This section looks at how you can bring an Inclusive Design approach into your existing design or development process. It outlines eight activities that can help you to achieve this. Underlying reasons are presented for conducting research with people and the concept of the 'lead user' is described.

PEOPLE-CENTRED DESIGN

WHAT IT IS: Consulting a diverse range of people to get different perspectives into your design and development process. Talking to people throughout all stages from ideation to validation. Older and disabled people can form a key component of this but other groups can also be consulted. It is important to have in-depth engagement, to research in context and see the issues from other people's point of view.

WHAT IT IS NOT: Designing for yourself, consulting only your friends or colleagues, talking to just the target market, holding a focus group at the office, designing with people in mind rather than actually speaking to them. Designing based on marketing data or statistics or just talking to a random sample of people to validate your ideas at the end.

Conducting research with people can help you go beyond functional problem-solving. Users can inspire you, inform creative thinking and drive innovation. They should be seen as valued partners and contributors to your process and be treated with dignity and respect.

This approach can give you direct access to consumer attitude and help you to understand lifestyle and aspirational factors. It can bring statistical information to life and support existing marketing data that you may have already gathered. As a business tool, people-centred design can enable you to innovate from the customer's perspective and use design more effectivley.

You do not have to work with a large sample of people to get meaningful insights. Six to 12 carefully selected people can be enough.

Adults with infants often only have one hand available

People with hearing impairments can assess visual and auditory information

Visually impaired individuals can test visual characteristics

Blind people can comment on tactile and auditory qualities

People with dementia can decide how intuitive and understandable a solution is. Older people can test a range of factors

Right: Lead user in an extreme context for the sports industry

LEAD USERS

Lead users are people who make greater demands on a product, system, service or environment and therefore challenge it in ways beyond that of the average, mainstream user.

While it is important not to ignore mainstream users or your selected target market, working with lead users can help to explore the limits of existing designs and provide the inspiration to develop new thinking. They can give you different insights than those obtained from your mainstream users and help to lead design development in new and undiscovered directions.

Because they make greater demands of a design, they often have to work around the limitations, revealing valuable, tacit knowledge and providing detailed insight into what doesn't work. If a design can stand up to the demands of a lead user then this can translate into a better design for everyone.

In Inclusive Design, people may be considered lead users for any number of reasons. This will depend on the nature of the design, what you are interested in exploring and the context of use. For example, if examining usability, a suitable lead user may have reduced physical ability such as poor eyesight, dexterity or hearing.

It is also important to consider other aspects that may make a person a lead user. This may have more to do with their lifestyle or cultural background, or the fact that they use the design to a high level or in an extreme context.

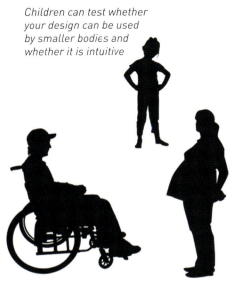

Children can test whether your design can be used by smaller bodies and whether it is intuitive

People with mobility problems can test physical accessibility

LEAD USER	TYPE OF INFORMATION THEY MAY PROVIDE
OLDER PEOPLE	intuitive, functional, aesthetics, strength, flexibility
DISABLED PEOPLE	visual, audible, tactile, strength, grip, accessible, functional
CHILDREN	intuitive, small bodies, strength, coordination, aesthetics
CULTURAL DIVERSITY	aesthetics, symbolism, value, function, context of use
MALE AND FEMALE	aesthetics, intuitive, strength, form, function

Above: This list is not exhaustive – think about who would be most relevant to your project

"People are experts in their own lives"

CHOOSING THE RIGHT LEAD USERS

Think differently and pick people who will provoke new ideas or be challenging to design for.
For instance:
- If you are designing wayfinding, appropriate lead users might have poor vision, be a tourist or have mobility problems
- If you are designing a bathroom, lead users might include older people, children, hospital patients or even prisoners. All of these would have an interesting perspective on hygiene or bathing
- If you are designing an online shopping service, some lead users might be people who are addicted to shopping or those who hate it. Both these extreme points of view will give alternative perspectives
- If you are designing a city square, lead users could include skateboarders, travellers with luggage, parents with prams, workers on a lunch break, unemployed individuals or street artists

It is important to choose lead users that are relevant to the design and its intended purpose. For example a small child may not be a suitable lead user for a razor, unless you are interested in child-safety features.

Within any lead user group, there can be wide variance in ability and individuals will therefore challenge the design in different ways. For example, in the visually impaired community only a small percentage of people are totally blind. This group might inform tactile solutions whilst the majority, who can see something, can talk about legibility as well.

Aim to choose lead users that are motivated and good at communicating their experiences. Children, people with cognitive impairment, dementia patients and autistic individuals may find it difficult to give feedback on a design. However, if it is important to consult them, it will be necessary to adapt the way in which you gather information.

Once parameters have been established for selecting lead users, it is best to aim for a variety within those parameters. For example, if older people are selected as lead users, make sure you have a mix of gender, social circumstance, culture and age within the group.

Lead users can be brought into the design process at any point from ideation through to validation. They can be especially relevant at the start of the project to give early feedback on direction and help to generate new ideas.

However, lead users can even be consulted when the project is undefined to help uncover radically different directions right at the start. Be creative and do not just use them to evaluate your ideas at the end of a project.

"Seeing one interesting thing from one user can be enough to get started"

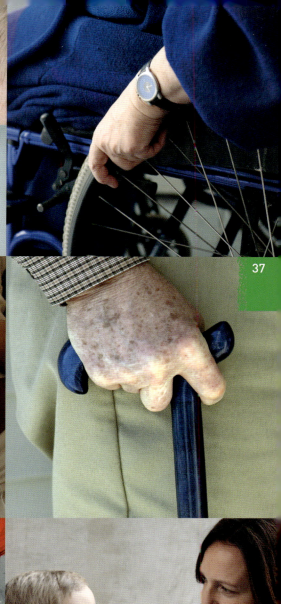

TIPS

- Remember it is not about designing specifically for a particular lead user. You will exclude a wider audience by designing for their specific needs. You are getting insights from them that can then be turned into mainstream solutions

- This is about learning from a qualitative experience not a quantitative one. Use fewer lead users and go into detail with them

- A lead user in one situation may be an average user in another

- Beware of expert users. Using the same person over and over again can turn them into an expert where they assess your design skills rather than give insights into their life

- Users will tell you what they think you want to hear

- Not all insights are valid. You will need to take out those that are. You are interpreting what lead users say and translating this into design ideas

- Do not choose users that you are personally close to as this can give biased results

COMPARING APPROACHES

Number-centred techniques are useful but people-centred research can add value to them. It can give deeper insight into consumer behaviour and bring marketing data to life.

The table below compares people-centred methods of research with number-centred methods. Number-centred methods, in this context, represent statistically-driven approaches to gathering information or traditional market research where hundreds or thousands of people are asked the same set of questions and the results then collected together to generate percentages.

Number-centred techniques have value but people-centred research can work alongside them to give insight into consumer behaviour. They also provide a qualitative evidence-base for any business interested in developing new ideas or innovative thinking. Market segmentation defines people according to how you want to see them, but people-centred techniques allow them to express themselves.

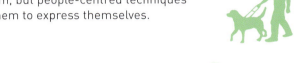

NUMBER-CENTRED RESEARCH	PEOPLE-CENTRED RESEARCH
Statistical results	Inspirational stories
Limited to a set of questions	Freedom to explore through dialogue
Reported life	Real life
Second-hand information	First-hand observation
Out of context	In context
Hear about issues	See issues
Market defined by segment	Person describes themselves
Actions or attitudes logged	Emotions and aspirations explored
Validate direction and limit focus	Open new possibilities
General trends	Individual thinking
Person is the subject of research	Person is the centre of research
Charts, numbers, percentages	Images, video, audio

THE DESIGN PROCESS

Most companies have a design or development process that they use to bring new ideas to market. Inclusive Design can be integrated into these models adding the value of a people-centred approach without disrupting existing practice.

There are many different ways of modelling a typical design development or innovation process and each company is likely to have developed their own version to suit their particular purpose or industry. However, each model will generally follow the same basic steps. This section introduces eight Inclusive Design elements and explains how they can be incorporated into the various stages of any process.

The design development model below is used by the Norwegian Design Council as a general example. It has a primary focus on the early phases in the process named the Ideation Stage in the diagram. This stage is of key importance in innovation projects as many of the decisions made here will impact the rest of the project. The activities grouped under the Ideation Stage can be iteratively used until a concept is defined and selected for development. It is then passed into the Operative Stage which is more linear and focuses on bringing the idea to market.

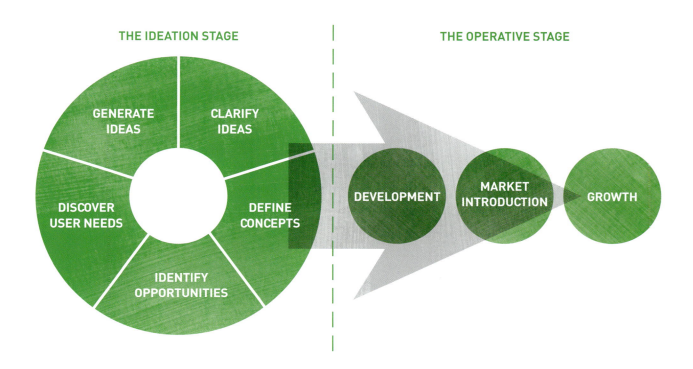

DEVELOPMENT PROCESS

Two other examples of project development processes are shown above. They are used in a variety of different industries but have been generalised to demonstrate typical practice. The process structures are similar as they share common phases. You should be able to recognise these stages within your own process though wording, number of stages and other details may differ.

For simplicity this book uses the the four stage model shown below with the Explore, Focus, Develop and Deliver stages.

INCLUSIVE DESIGN ACTIVITIES

The eight Inclusive Design activities described on pages 42-51 give you an overview of practical methods and techniques for bringing Inclusive Design thinking into your development process. Each activity consists of tasks that help to bring the user into focus.

In the early stages, these activities include methods for setting up your research, obtaining insights from users and then using these insights as inspiration for ideas. In the later stages, as a project progresses through its development cycles, the activities help to maintain a people-centred perspective during decision-making and evaluation.

It is important that the tasks are adapted to suit your own needs and individual process. It may not be necessary to complete every activity, or even follow the order shown on pages 42-43. They can be used as appropriate. These activities should not be seen as standalone tasks but eventually become an integral part of your own development process.

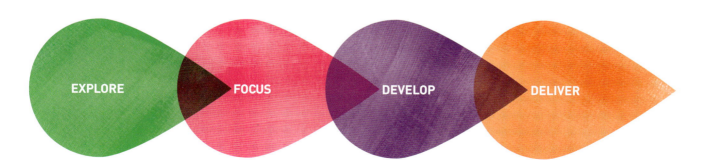

Above: A generic four-stage design process. This is used to explain the Inclusive Design activities on the following pages

CRITERIA TOOL

Criteria tools are often used throughout the development process to check whether ideas meet certain objectives or are of a good standard. They are a way of making decisions or ranking ideas.

WHAT

The criteria tool is a decision-making tool that keeps the perspective of the user in focus throughout the design process. Criteria are drawn up based on initial insights gathered from user research and are combined with the commercial objectives set for the project. These criteria then help to define the key requirements a successful design must fulfil and set a framework for measuring the success of a particular idea.

Ideas are scored and ranked on a quantitative scale for each criteria allowing you to assess and prioritise those that best fulfill the needs of the user and the project. Used iteratively and throughout the design process the criteria tool will help to compare ideas, check their performance and show areas for improvement.

HOW

1. Define the sequence of interactions between the user and the design. Remember to include the entire relationship from start to finish. For a product this may begin from the decision to buy until the product is discarded. For a service this may be from finding the service to termination or renewal.

2. Produce a set of criteria for each stage in this sequence that are important from the users' perspective. This should include both functional and emotional experience. The criteria can then be weighted in relation to each other depending on how critical it is to success. This weighting may take into account factors such as the effect on cost or how broadly across the market the effect applies.

3. Create a visual scale that allows you to record and clearly show how well a solution scores compared with another.

4. Refine the criteria tool to become more specific and focused as the design and development progresses. During later stages, your criteria tool can be refined to focus on a particular concept or scenario.

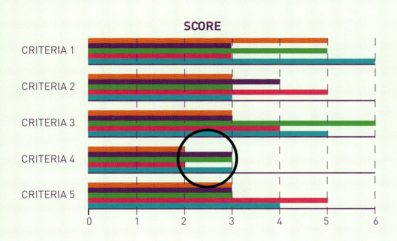

Lead users:
- Older person
- Visually impaired
- Person with arthritis
- Child
- Person without capability loss

Left: Criteria tool where a range of users have rated each criteria on a scale of 1 to 6. The low score on criteria 4 shows opportunity for improvement as circled

ADDING INCLUSIVE DESIGN TO YOUR DESIGN PROCESS

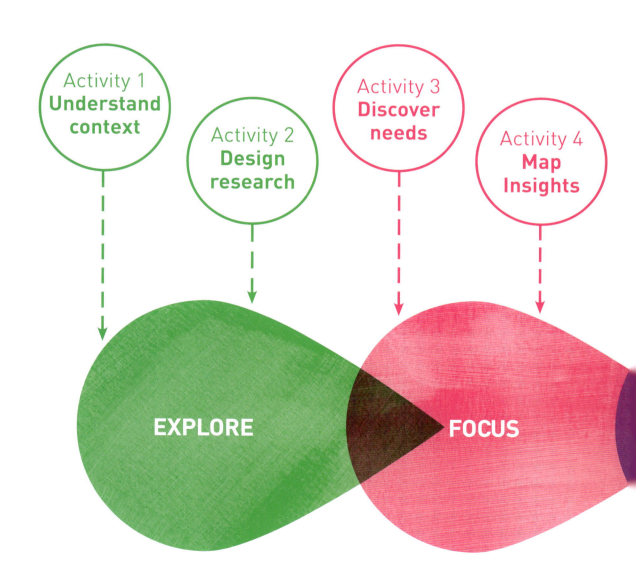

This diagram shows a typical development process. At each stage there are a number of Inclusive Design activities that can be added to create a more people-centred approach. Adapt to suit your purpose. Each activity is described in detail on the following pages.

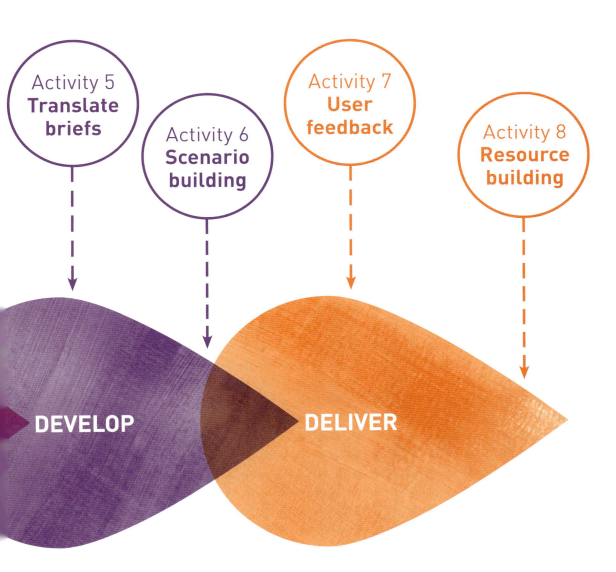

ACTIVITY 1
UNDERSTAND CONTEXT

This activity will give you a better understanding of the context surrounding the issue that you are looking at. It will give you a firm basis for moving forward as well as people-inspired insights and direction.

Before starting any project it is important to understand the market in which you are operating and have an idea of the overall landscape from your users' perspective. This will help you to build a correct vision for your project, see how you can improve existing offers and ensure that your initial ideas have relevance to the real world. Spending time on this and getting it right will give you good grounding for the rest of the process.

METHODS

- **Literature search**: See what information already exists. You could look at trends, web research, books, academic publications and current media.
- **Market research**: Find out who is affected by your context. Examine marketing data, statistics, surveys and information gathered from large numbers of people.
- **Competitor audit**: Find out which other companies are operating in this field. Look at existing designs to identify gaps in the market and analyse current solutions. Looking at parallel industries can show you how other sectors have responded.
- **Initial user visits or observation**: See how people behave within the existing context. Explore their experiences and identify key areas of interest. You can do this through web forums, telephone interviews or natural observation. (See pages 58-63)
- **Go into the context**: Explore the issues firsthand. Learn about the situation by experiencing it yourself. Use your own products or services and talk to other people who also interface with them such as the sales team, the distributors and end users.

END RESULT

By completing this activity you will define areas for research focus that have captured your attention. You can then set up clear project goals and have some idea of how to approach your issue. You will also be able to assess whether you have correctly understood your context and adjust accordingly. You will be able to scope other opportunities that you might not have seen before.

ACTIVITY 2
DESIGN RESEARCH

Your research should aim to get a significant amount of insights from the users you decide to work with. Spend time planning this carefully as badly designed research will produce limited results and not be cost-effective.

It is important to allow adequate time to design your research properly as this will give you the best chance of success and ensure that common mistakes are avoided. Building on your understanding of the context, think about the type of information you will need, how you can access it and who you will get it from. Consider the availability of the users, your timeframe and budget, then plan accordingly.

METHODS

- **Ask the question**: Identify the primary research question. Audit your existing insights, rank them and select those with most potential. Turn your insights into a question. For example if your insight is: "76 year old Berit gets her son to put up her new shelves", your question might be: "why don't older people like power tools?"

- **Find the focus**: Identify and map key issues. Understand the different aspects of your research question and explore all angles. You could use a mind map, lists, brainstorming and other creative methods. In the example above, you might consider issues such as: Are the tools too heavy? Is she worried about safety? Or do the shelves actually give her an opportunity to see her son?

- **Create the framework**: Develop criteria for finding users. This could be a simple x-y graph, chart or table. In the example, you could look at differences in age, gender and familiarity with power tools.

- **Pick your users**: Identify potential lead users (see pages 35-37) and their position on your framework. Aim for contrast and variety. In the example above, your framework could include looking at older adults who have never used power tools and those who are familiar with them.

END RESULT

This activity will give you a solid basis for conducting research with people and a way of taking this forward. Themes for exploration should be organised into a research framework and you will have developed criteria for selecting users. Your research methods will be defined and designed.

URBAN   RURAL

SINGLE   COUPLE

LOCAL FAMILY   DISPERSED FAMILY

ACTIVITY 3
DISCOVER NEEDS

This is the point where you put your planning into action and go out to work with users. You are immersing yourself in other people's lives and aiming to understand their problems, needs, desires and aspirations.

There are many techniques that you can use in this activity to get closer to your users and meaningfully engage with them. These are covered in greater detail under the Research Methods section (pages 52-73). Although you are looking to capture insights, do not treat people like test subjects. Ensure that your users are seen as valued contributors and are respected. The insights you gather will be a platform for inspiration in the next activity.

METHODS

- **Scheduling**: Contact your users and arrange to meet. Make sure you are fully prepared, that the users have signed consent forms where necessary and your activities with them are fully explained.
- **Going and doing**: Conducting the user visits and research. Techniques might include questionnaires, web forums, observation (both natural and controlled), interviews, research kits and workshops (see pages 52-73).
- **Research focus**: Keep the primary question in mind but also allow yourself to look beyond it. For instance, gathering information on the context can reveal hidden information that is relevant to the research focus.
- **Tune method**: Do not be afraid to change your plan or review the primary question. If you are not finding out the information you need or if new exciting directions are opening up, modify your plan to suit. Build on each experience.

END RESULT

Completing this activity should produce large amounts of data containing rich insights and qualitative information from the people you have worked with. You need to capture and store this in an organised way for later access and analysis. Do not be overwhelmed at this point by the amount of user data that you might have gathered.

ACTIVITY 4
MAP INSIGHTS

Having gathered insights from people, you now need to map them. Review and analyse all the information to identify key themes and opportunities. Extracting the right insights will lead to new ideas or designs.

You need to make sense of the research data you have gathered. Not everything will be relevant. Sort those insights that are inconsequential from those that are important or inspiring. Refer back to the primary question to help filter results. Do not be afraid to discard things that are not of interest.

METHODS

- **Review data**: Get an overview on all data gathered. See what you have captured and analyse gaps. Conduct further research if those gaps need to be filled. Review photographs, videos, interviews to separate insightful information from background information.
- **Organise data:** Sort the data into groups. Create a method that will give you and your team easy access. Back-up and keep information that you might not need for this project. It might be useful in other projects.
- **Visualise data**: Search for patterns and themes. Lay out everything you have chosen so you can contrast and compare. Look for natural groupings, common themes and cross-references to help you organise. Be visual and qualitative in the way you visualise. Do not just use lists or spreadsheets. Use alternative mapping tools.
- **Rank data**: Prioritise needs and findings. Develop a list of criteria to rank insights that respond to the primary question (see page 41 for a criteria tool). You might find that your research opens up other opportunities so rephrase the primary question if necessary. Be strict in prioritising your results. Brainstorm with other people who are not connected to the project – fresh eyes can be very helpful.

END RESULT
At the end of this activity, you should have some new discoveries with an evidence-base of human stories. These could be issues, problems or interesting solutions discovered during the user research. These can act as starting points for idea generation and design briefs. They can be quite broad at this stage but will soon lead to specific design directions. At this time you will have an understanding of key themes and issues.

ACTIVITY 5
TRANSLATE BRIEFS

This activity takes the ranked ideas or themes from the last activity and translates them into design briefs to be addressed. Choose those directions with the most potential and define the challenges to overcome.

Create design briefs that take account of the evidence-base that you have generated and reference the original project goal or mission. Build on ideas that have the most potential for your business. You can bring other colleagues into the brief-writing process for alternative perspectives. Make sure that you maintain the user voice in the briefs that you write including direct quotes if necessary.

METHODS

– **Success criteria**: Build a list of criteria for the brief. These will be important in assessing the success of the outcomes and can be used to evaluate and select ideas throughout the design phase.

– **Write briefs**: Define the goals or challenges to overcome. Be very specific as to the topic of each brief. For example, do not write 'my idea will improve people's lives'. Write 'my idea will aim to get schoolchildren to drink more water to improve their concentration'. You should be able to summarise your brief in two or three sentences.

– **Choose briefs**: Select briefs for development. Use the list of criteria developed to choose those briefs with the most potential.

END RESULT

This activity will give you specific briefs to respond to that explore different creative directions. This is the start of the traditional development process but it will now have a people-centred evidence-base to give it a more solid foundation. At this stage, your briefs and design directions will be driven by your users, helping to ensure that you are answering the right question.

ACTIVITY 6
SCENARIO BUILDING

This activity complements the traditional idea-generation phase of the typical design process. Use the research you have gathered to build scenarios that will help you to see things from the point of view of your users.

Scenario building will help you to keep in mind the insights already gathered from your users and ensure that their needs and aspirations are driving the process. Generate ideas in response to those scenarios and virtually test ideas from a particular user's perspective. This will allow you to assess which ideas will work much earlier on in the process.

METHODS

- **User profiles**: Determine main drivers and character traits of each user. Think about what is important to each individual and summarise key aspects of their personality.
- **Personas**: Generate fictional characters based on your research and on real users. You should have a good idea how they might think and respond to situations they face.
- **Storyboarding**: Visualise scenarios to explore an idea. Draw out sequences of how and where the idea might potentially be used. It is important to give detail to the central characters and the context.
- **Role-play**: See from the user's point of view. Imagine that you are the user and act out scenarios reacting as you think they would. Use other team members to help or set in the real world context.
- **Revisit insight databank**: Keep the user study fresh in your mind. Remind and re-inspire yourself throughout the idea generation phase using the data gathered during the research.

END RESULT

Completing this activity should generate a range of concepts, ideas and scenarios that are driven by user need whilst considering other factors that are important in business. It will help you to answer the brief in new and interesting ways, animating solutions and testing them from a user perspective.

ACTIVITY 7
USER FEEDBACK

Evaluation with users should happen iteratively throughout the development process, but at this stage, as the design is nearing completion, users should be brought in to give specific feedback on the ideas produced.

Once concepts have been developed into realistic solutions and other constraints such as materials and manufacturing have been addressed, final validation should take place. Realistic prototypes or mock-ups should be tested with a range of users to verify design solutions, record initial market reaction and fine tune details (see pages 72-73). Leave time within the overall process to make final adjustments to your design as a result of user feedback.

METHODS

- **Test onsite**: Ask users to come to your office to test prototypes. They can do this individually or in focus groups. Capturing feedback will be easier but you will not see the prototypes being used in a real context.
- **Test offsite**: People take away prototypes to test in a real context or over an extended period of time. This can give a more realistic picture but can be more difficult to capture feedback.
- **Research methods**: Reuse the research methods you have applied earlier in the process (see pages 52-73) but re-apply with new focus. You are not using them to capture insights but to evaluate concepts.
- **Mass market**: Test outside your lead user group to assess wider market appeal. Bring in a variety of mainstream users.

END RESULT

This activity will allow you to verify your design solutions and test the details, usability and features. It makes sure that user need is informing the design right up to the point at which it is ready for production. This will help to deliver a more market-ready, considered outcome. You will also pick up on early failings and be able to design them out.

ACTIVITY 8
RESOURCE BUILDING

Collect and keep all the information and insights that you have gathered even those that were not used for this particular project. Material collected along the way may have relevance to other areas of your business.

As a result of your activities with users, you will have knowledge and experience that can be passed onto other projects and colleagues. This should be organised and stored in a way that can be easily accessed either physically or digitally. Your studies with lead users can act as a resource and reference for future projects and help to create a library of user data for your organisation. Information that might not have been applicable to one project could be vital for another so make sure you save discarded data.

METHODS

- **Image library**: Collect and organise still and video images by theme or keyword in a manner that makes it easy for other people to search and access. Do not upload all your raw data. Edit and select the material that is most interesting and relevant.
- **Insight database**: Create a database of insights gathered throughout your research. This can be quotes from users, ideas you have had or problems that have been articulated.
- **Persona library**: Creating personas based on real users can help to generate more inclusive briefs and virtually test ideas in other projects. Make sure that the personas you create are believable and have depth to their character. Write in likes and dislikes as well as physical functionality for example.
- **Catalogue unexplored ideas**: Often user research will uncover other ideas that are new and exciting but not relevant to the brief you are addressing. Record these ideas for consideration at a future date. They might be a potential fit for another project.

END RESULT
At the end of this activity you will have a reference library of people-centred insights in the form of quotes, pictures and video. This information can be a valuable resource for your organisation in developing new projects as well as maintaining an Inclusive Design approach. The innovation that results from this process can also add value from your clients' perspective. However, most importantly, completing this activity means that you do not have to start from scratch the next time.

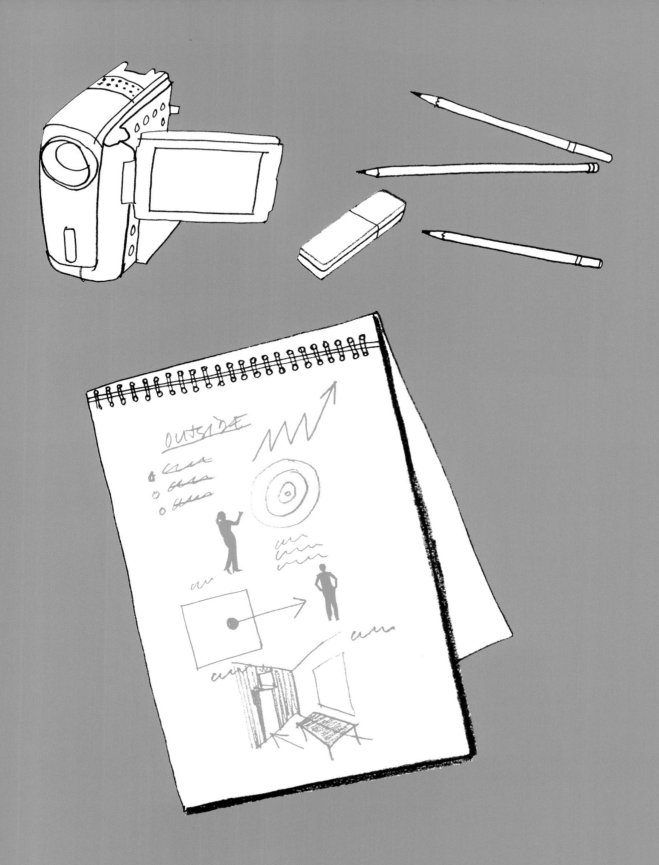

TOOLS

This section gives you practical advice on using nine different tools for conducting research with people. There are low, medium and high contact methods that reflect different levels of engagement and resources needed. Each tool is outlined giving strengths, weaknesses and useful tips to help you in the field.

RESEARCH TOOLS

These tools and techniques enable you to conduct research with people. These can be used even if you have little or no experience. The nine research tools outlined here will help you to gather insights and feedback effectively. They are not just for designers, but can be used by anyone.

INTRODUCTION

There are many different research methods and they all have varying strengths, weaknesses, levels of user involvement and resource requirements. This section outlines nine methods describing how, when and why you might use them. Not all methods will suit every purpose or be applicable to all users. For example, group interviews are not suitable for those with poor hearing and web surveys cannot be answered if the respondent does not have access to a computer.

The table below arranges the research methods into categories of low, medium and high contact. This ranks them according to a number of factors:

1. The degree of interaction with the user.
2. The depth to which insights can be explored.
3. Time and resources needed to prepare your research.

For example, natural observation, where you observe people's behaviour without talking to them, has little interaction with the user and as a result the depth to which any observed insight can be explored is also low. This is not to say that the insights gathered are any less important but this method is more suited to discovering insights rather than examining them deeply.

There are no fixed rules as to when methods should be used but low contact tools tend to be used at the beginning of the development process, medium contact throughout and high contact in the middle and at the end. Most of the methods can be used in combination with each other. For example a visit to a user's home may combine a questionnaire with an interview or controlled observation with a specific task. You should decide how and when to use the methods to suit the type of information you require.

TIPS ON CONDUCTING RESEARCH

- Set your research goals. Think about the scope of the project and what you are trying to find out. This can help to select the right method
- Adapt your techniques. Use this guide as a framework and adapt each study according to the user and the focus of the project. This can range from taking into account a potential user's disability or developing a new method to capture a particular type of information
- Always get consent from people when recording them
- Make users comfortable and inform them about how you intend to use the information you are collecting
- Do not forget that your users are people who are helping you. Thank them and recognise them as partners in the process

LOW CONTACT	MEDIUM CONTACT	HIGH CONTACT
Questionnaire	Interview	Controlled observation
Web forum	Research kit	Workshop
Natural observation	Design provocation	Evaluation

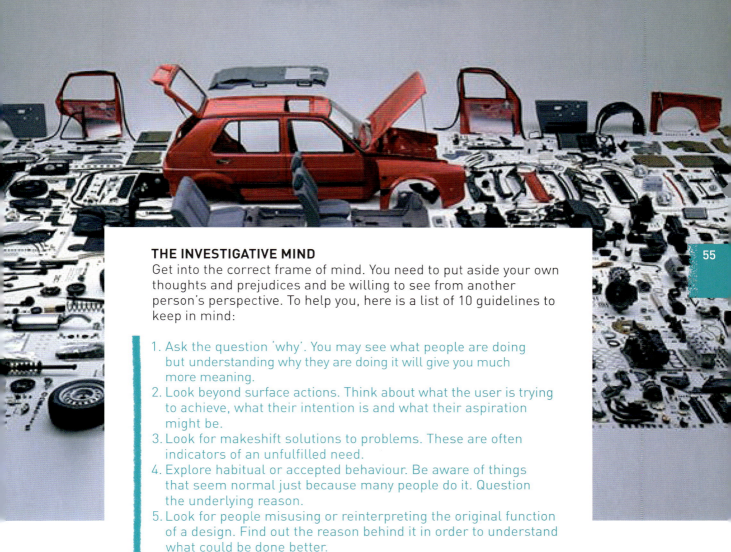

THE INVESTIGATIVE MIND

Get into the correct frame of mind. You need to put aside your own thoughts and prejudices and be willing to see from another person's perspective. To help you, here is a list of 10 guidelines to keep in mind:

1. Ask the question 'why'. You may see what people are doing but understanding why they are doing it will give you much more meaning.
2. Look beyond surface actions. Think about what the user is trying to achieve, what their intention is and what their aspiration might be.
3. Look for makeshift solutions to problems. These are often indicators of an unfulfilled need.
4. Explore habitual or accepted behaviour. Be aware of things that seem normal just because many people do it. Question the underlying reason.
5. Look for people misusing or reinterpreting the original function of a design. Find out the reason behind it in order to understand what could be done better.
6. Pay attention to things that people have difficulty with. It is likely that others will also face the same problem.
7. Do not just focus on the subject matter. Also consider the context as this can influence results. Think about time of day, location or ambient noises for example.
8. Examine interactions such as the relationships between people, and between people and objects.
9. Be aware of the whole process that a user follows leading up to and beyond your particular event of interest.

LOW CONTACT
1. QUESTIONNAIRE

A list of questions sent to users to find out what they think or feel about particular issues. Can be printed or emailed.

WHEN

Usually used in the early stages to identify issues and areas for further research

ISSUES

- Choose the right type of question to get the type of information you want, i.e. structured, semi-structured or open questions
- The format needs to reflect the type of answer required for each question
- Decide on a delivery method, whether it will be completed online, sent by email or post, or whether the investigator will be present

STRENGTHS

- A relatively quick and cost effective way to reach a large number of users
- Good for access to users who may live far away or for those who wish to remain anonymous
- The standardised format makes it suitable for comparison between different users
- Both quantitative and qualitative information can be gathered. You can ask for written responses or tick boxes
- A good way of getting a broad overview of a subject where no other information is available

WEAKNESSES

- Leading questions can bias responses
- It is hard to predict or control the response rate
- Explanations cannot be given to a user who does not understand a question unless the investigator is present
- Questionnaires can seem impersonal, making users less likely to engage
- No access to observable context or behaviour and responses are limited to things of which a user is conscious
- The information gathered can be dry or uninspiring and not visually compelling

HOW

1. Find people willing to participate and include an introduction to the study along with your questionnaire to give them context.
2. Consider the needs of your users when writing the questionnaire. For example those who are not computer literate or are visually impaired will have different requirements.
3. Aim for the questionnaire to take approximately 10-20 minutes to complete.
4. Trial the questionnaire with a colleague first then edit it to improve the clarity and ease of use.
5. Focus on the topics that interest you. Do not try to cover everything or the user will lose interest.
6. Make the questions simple and clear. Avoid negatives in the question as these may bias the response.
7. Use tick boxes, scales, ranks and charts to reduce writing tasks.
8. Formatting is very important. Think about the sequence of questions, break them into sections and use pictures where appropriate. Indicate the type of response expected for each section.
9. Send the questionnaire to more people than you require as the response rate is unpredictable. Quantitative surveys require a larger sample to achieve meaningful results.
10. Use an online questionnaire maker where appropriate as these can manage and sort the data for you.

GOES WELL WITH

- Interviews: A questionnaire can serve as a topic guide for an interview or a basis for a follow-up interview allowing the users responses to be explored in greater detail
- Research kits: A questionnaire can be included as part of a research kit to gather background information

BEST SUITED TO

- Gaining a broad overview of a topic and asking preliminary questions to prepare for further investigation
- Gathering quantitative evidence to support further investigation
- Getting information on specific topics where no other information exists

LOW CONTACT
2. WEB FORUM

The investigator posts questions on a web forum for members to respond to or reads existing posts that people have already written.

STRENGTHS

- A relatively quick and low cost way of reaching many people within a community that may already be interested in your topic
- People are likely to engage and respond to your questions as web forums are already there for discussion
- You can ask targetted questions and find a rich supply of information on a specific topic

WEAKNESSES

- No opportunity to observe behaviour or context firsthand
- Users are anonymous and responses cannot be verified
- Over-enthusiastic forum members may lead the discussion away from your topic
- Impossible to gauge the response rate and it might take some time for people to get back to you
- Knowledge of user is limited to answers on a specific theme unless further information is sought privately

WHEN

Used during the formative phases or to target specific user groups

ISSUES

- Decide whether you want people to respond privately to you or publicly to the rest of the forum
- Make sure your questions are appropriate for the forum and within the rules of conduct. Get permission for any activities you perform or any information that you use
- Decide whether you require anecdotal responses or a survey with 'yes' or 'no' answers

HOW

1. Search for forums online that deal with your subject of interest. Be sure to read existing threads on similar topics first. This can help to find out the information currently available and prevent you posting the same questions again.

2. Get permission from the forum administrator where necessary and adhere to forum rules.

3. Be honest about your presence. For example do not pretend to be over 65 if you are not.

4. Forums are well suited to qualitative responses so try to ask questions such as "does anyone have a problem with..." or "what do you think about..."

5. If appropriate, post pictures relevant to the subject matter to help drive the discussion.

6. Only cover a few topics within the general forum. If people are interested in the discussion, start a new thread.

7. If people are willing, it can be useful to contact them privately and explore their answers in greater depth. People may also be more willing to provide photographs and better contextual information.

8. Record the discussions and responses along with any photographs.

BEST SUITED TO

- Finding out specific information at the early stages to understand the issues before going out into the field

- Gathering real-world insights and personal stories from people to build an evidence base for your approach

- Making use of established expertise and experience and talking to many individuals at the same time

LOW CONTACT
3. NATURAL OBSERVATION

Observing people in their natural setting with no interference from the investigator to see how users actually behave within a given context.

WHEN

Used during the exploratory phase or to gather key insights into general behaviour

ISSUES

- It is important to remain unnoticed. The investigator must take care not to be intrusive and make people uncomfortable

- Choose locations to observe rather than specific people to follow. It is a criminal offence in some countries to follow people without their permission

- Observe group behaviour rather than focusing on any individual. Use in public spaces rather than private areas. Do not stalk, stare, use telephoto lens or do anything else which might be illegal or disrespectful

STRENGTHS

- Gives honest and insightful information. The user is acting in a natural context and is not influenced in any way

- Can uncover behaviour of which you were not previously aware

- Can reveal surprising or unexpected events

- Can capture ordinary interactions between people, products, services and environments

- Good for seeing surrounding contextual information

- Will create visual data to act as inspiration

- Requires little preparation time and can be started at short notice

WEAKNESSES

- Cannot guarantee a specific event will occur

- Time consuming to conduct. You might have to sit for several hours in a particular place

- Time consuming to analyse and reveal insights. You may have to review images or video later to notice additional insights

- Users are not interviewed so the investigator could misinterpret what they see

- Cannot capture user personality or history beyond the observed duration

- Confined to public spaces which will allow you to take photographs or video

- Difficult to observe vulnerable groups such as children

HOW

1. Choose a location that relates to your research topic and observe how people act within that space.

2. Be prepared to stay in one location for several hours. Between 1-2 hours is enough to provide some meaningful information or indicate whether the location is suitable.

3. Pay attention to the context, even information that may not seem important at the time. Try to record points of interest, time intervals, sketch layouts, floor plans, movements and dynamics.

4. Take a still camera or video camera where allowed. You can capture complex situations in great detail and examine them later.

5. Have your camera on and ready as important events may happen at a moment's notice.

6. If the observation is task-based, then participate. You will experience the context firsthand and blend in with other people.

BEST SUITED TO

– Forming an opinion quickly on a large topic such as looking at the problems people have whilst travelling through the city

– Gathering insight on general behaviour, actions, interactions, procedure and context rather than gaining specific information from individuals

MEDIUM CONTACT
1. INTERVIEW

Conversation between the investigator and the user or expert. Questions are asked by the investigator and responses given by the person being interviewed.

WHEN

Generally used during the initial phases of a project but can be of value throughout the design process

ISSUES

- Decide on a formal or informal tone. For a formal interview, develop a list of structured questions. In an informal interview you allow the conversation to develop naturally
- If possible, choose a location that is relevant to the user or the project focus, such as their home or workplace, so that you can see them in context
- Interviewing several people at once can be useful to assess group dynamics but the group must be well known to each other to get useful information. The conversation needs to be controlled to give equal opportunity to everyone

STRENGTHS

- Relatively quick
- Good access to the personality of the user
- The conversation can be directed by the investigator and refocused if necessary
- Good depth of information achievable
- Good access to people's aspirations and emotional reactions
- Users can show or respond to objects that are relevant to the interview
- Investigator can gauge body language

TELEPHONE SPECIFIC ISSUES
An interview can also be conducted over the telephone but there are some pros and cons to be aware of:

- You can access remote users or those wanting anonymity
- There is no way to observe reactions or read body language
- Some people may prefer to speak by phone while others may open up better in person

WEAKNESSES

- Can be time-consuming to arrange interviews
- Relies heavily on quality of the questions and personality of the interviewer
- Questions can be leading and you may influence the response. Users will sometimes give you the answer they think you want to hear
- Limited value for comparative studies. You cannot give every user exactly the same interview
- Limited to insights and issues of which the user is conscious and able to verbalise. You only hear what they say rather than see what they do
- Recordings can be lengthy to analyse

HOW

1. Introduce yourself and your project before conducting the interview to prepare the user. This may be done via email, an initial telephone call, or through a third party.
2. Arrange a time for the interview when both parties are available to commit some time and talk freely.
3. Try to choose a location that is not too noisy or distracting and affords a level of privacy.
4. Aim for between 6 to 12 interviews. Interviewing small numbers of people can yield good results.
5. Do not rush but try to keep the interviews short. Between 15 minutes and two hours is usually enough.
6. Prepare a topic guide or a list of questions to help you to cover the important areas and remember to ask them.
7. Start by asking general questions about the user and their lifestyle. Try to understand who they are. This will help to build a context for their answers and be useful when comparing responses from different people.
8. Do not be too rigid with your plan. Aim to lead the conversation to explore important topics but allow the user to answer freely.
9. Ask people to explain answers further if you want more detail.
10. Record the conversation where possible using audio or video as it is difficult to interview and take notes at the same time. Always get permission. Never put the camera between you and the person being interviewed as this creates a barrier.
11. Set aside some time immediately after each interview to make notes and general comments while they are fresh in your mind. This can save you hours of trying to remember the most interesting or important things later.

GOES WELL WITH

- Provocation: allow users to respond to pictures, prototypes and props
- Questionnaire: can serve as a useful topic guide
- Controlled observation: ask the user to perform a task and interview them about the experience

BEST SUITED TO

- Investigations into a specific topic area to gather details where no other information is available
- Gaining an in-depth understanding of individual people
- Getting technical information or opinions from experts

MEDIUM CONTACT
2. RESEARCH KIT

Users are asked to complete research kits prepared by the investigator in order to capture information about their lives. Tasks and activities may include diaries, timelines, question cards, disposable cameras, mapping and drawing.

WHEN

Used during the formative and exploratory phases. Can be used to generate design directions

ISSUES

- Decide whether users should complete in their own time or while the investigator is present
- Depending on the individual, some people may easily engage while others may see it as a burden

STRENGTHS

- Can cover an extended period of time
- Can capture information when it is not possible for the investigator to be present or in private areas such as bedrooms and bathrooms
- Good for capturing information about the lifestyle, personality and preferences of individual users
- Provides a good mixture of qualitative and quantitative insights
- Allows time for a person to reflect on an issue and give richer feedback
- Good for creating visual data for inspiration and will give you material that can be used as an evidence base for decisions

WEAKNESSES

- Very reliant on the motivation and commitment of the user to complete the kit. Be prepared for a low response rate
- Badly designed or confusing kits will not be effective and produce limited results
- Insights can only be explored further when followed with an interview
- Time consuming to design and create an effective kit
- Time consuming to analyse and reveal insights from the information gathered
- Potentially slow to gather information
- Not suited to busy users

HOW

1. Keep the research kit as easy and quick as possible to complete. A complex and lengthy kit risks being rejected by the user.

2. To encourage people to accept and complete the kit, make it appealing and attractive. It can be helpful to include a small gift to say thank you.

3. Include an introduction and explanation of the project and make sure that your instructions are clear and concise.

4. Think about the type of information that you would like to capture and tailor the activities towards getting it.

5. Try to make the kit fun to complete. Keep writing tasks short and make it creative instead. Ask the user to fill in charts, draw or take pictures.

6. If you can, personally explain the kit to the user. Otherwise it can be helpful to include examples or suggestions to start them off.

7. Include an agreement form for them to sign and contact details where they can reach you should they have any questions.

8. Provide all necessary materials in the probe i.e. pens, paper, stickers or disposable cameras. The user should not have to source or buy anything.

9. If the user is to complete the probe in their own time give a firm deadline and include prepaid packaging with your address on it.

10. Due to the detailed amount of data to be gathered a small number of users is advised. Six to 12 will be optimal for most situations.

GOES WELL WITH

– Interview: interviewing the user beforehand will allow you to introduce subjects of interest and explain how to use the research kit. A follow-up interview after the kit has been completed will allow you to explore any insights further

BEST SUITED TO

– Capturing a broad picture of daily lives and context especially if research over a period of time is required

– Providing insights into an individual's personality and aspirations

– Providing access to subtle or hidden issues that a person might not typically be able to articulate or demonstrate in an interview

MEDIUM CONTACT
3. DESIGN PROVOCATION

Observing people in their natural setting with no interference from the investigator to see how users actually behave within a given context.

WHEN

During the early and middle stages of the design process to explore potential directions and create discussion around prospective ideas

ISSUES

- Decide whether you want the users to alter, influence or even create the provocation or to simply give feedback on it
- Construct as either a group or individual activity

STRENGTHS

- Can help stimulate discussion and inform new directions
- Can present users with untested, future-thinking or even unfeasible ideas for feedback early on in the development process
- People are able to relate better to physical objects and visuals than abstract ideas
- Asking the user to respond to a sketch prototype can reveal the motivation behind their choices
- Early assessment of acceptability of design concepts
- Engages a person's imagination and their own empathic response

WEAKNESSES

- People find it difficult to see beyond details. You might want them to comment on the concept direction but they get hung up on the colour
- Users are not generally trained in design so feedback must take account of this
- Ideas and discussion can be limited by the range of provocations shown
- Provocations may be too abstract for some users who need something more concrete to respond to

HOW

1. The investigator creates and brings a number of provocations to show to a user and ask for feedback.
2. Allow for as wide a range of provocations as possible in order to accommodate the subject being explored. Try not to be too conservative. This is an opportunity to push the boundaries.
3. Clearly explain the purpose of the provocation and what you hope to explore. For example are you interested in the form or function, or both?
4. Props can be used to help to discuss symbolic meaning as well as explore physical and tactile qualities. These are a selection of existing objects for the user to comment on.
5. Speculative designs can be explored by mixing or contrasting existing ideas. These are usually simple hybrid images or customisable sketches that allow people to create an ideal design for themselves.
6. Concept designs such as images, storyboards and sketch models can be shown to the user to help gauge responses and clarify needs.
7. Asking the user to explain their responses or decisions can help to understand motivations and potential design requirements.
8. Use the provocations as a starting point for discussion and feedback on designs and directions. Try not to get stuck on an assessment of the details.

GOES WELL WITH

- Interview: design provocations can be useful in an interview. They can add an extra layer of more specific feedback and help to focus discussion onto design issues
- Workshop: design provocations could be used as a creative activity or as a starting point for discussion within a workshop

BEST SUITED TO

- Focusing the design direction in the early stages of development
- Talking about ideas that users might not be able to understand or visualise without a physical piece to respond to
- Exploring a range of new ideas rather than finalising or validating
- Assessment and clarification of key features and requirements from a user perspective

HIGH CONTACT
1. CONTROLLED OBSERVATION

Observing people going about their normal activities with their consent. Presenting them with a task or design and observing how they complete or interact with it.

WHEN

Used during the exploratory phases and evaluative stages

ISSUES

- Choose the level of control. Are you observing the people performing everyday activities in their natural settings or are you introducing them to a new environment and asking them to complete specific tasks?

- Decide on whether the observation space is controlled or not, for example indoors or outdoors, public or private

- Choose level of interaction between observer and user. Decide how much the investigator may be involved or whether the user will be left on their own

STRENGTHS

- Can understand user intentions and opinions by asking them questions during the observation

- Can recreate or simulate specific events of interest

- The user can be asked to repeat specific actions

- Good for understanding and capturing the natural context and external influences on the user

- Can uncover insights that the user is not aware of themselves and then probe them further

- A good way of seeing and documenting procedures or observing how people respond to different situations

WEAKNESSES

- People tend to behave differently when they know they are being observed. You might not see their natural behaviour

- People can become self-conscious and skew responses

- Difficult to recreate complex or group interactions

- The way that a task or scenario is presented by the investigator can bias the response

- Time-consuming to conduct observation and gather information

- Time-consuming to analyse all the information gathered

- Can be difficult to record the observation using a still camera or video camera in certain locations or situations

HOW

1. Plan your strategy for conducting the observation. Will you observe people going about their everyday business or will you recreate or simulate a particular event and set them tasks to complete?

2. When shadowing, only participate if it does not distract or unduly influence the user.

3. When simulating an event or activity try to recreate natural conditions wherever possible. Choose your context and locations carefully.

4. Do not demonstrate when presenting tasks or scenarios for an individual to complete. They will then just do it in the way you have shown them.

5. Ask users to verbalise their thoughts during a task or process. This can help to understand their perceptions and decision-making.

6. When a user needs direction try to assist without prompting them.

7. Take a camera or preferably a video camera as it allows you to capture complex situations easily. Recordings can then be examined in greater detail at a later stage.

8. When videoing try to set up the camera in a location where it is obvious and will soon be forgotten by the user.

GOES WELL WITH

– Interview: finding out about the user's will help to contextualise the observed responses and encourage the user to give explanations

BEST SUITED TO

– Experiencing the user's daily life and capturing the broader context

– Detailed understanding of a specific task, context, or action from a user perspective

– Giving feedback on existing designs and activities

HIGH CONTACT
2. WORKSHOP

A group of users led by a moderator participate in discussion and exercises to explore a subject or design idea in greater detail. People can be asked questions or directed to perform tasks.

WHEN

Used during the early phases to gain broader understanding of a topic and during evaluative stages to define problems or test ideas

ISSUES

- Engaging and controlling a group of people is challenging and requires a skilled moderator who is energetic, able to focus the discussion and has good knowledge of the topic being discussed
- Good time management is crucial when dealing with groups of people working together
- It can be difficult to capture and make sense of the information generated as workshops can be energetic events with many people talking at the same time

STRENGTHS

- Can explore multiple points of view within the same discussion
- Group participation can stimulate new ideas as people bounce ideas off each other
- Explores contrasting ideas and opinions
- Highlights differing user experience and expertise
- Feedback on design directions will come from different perspectives
- Can produce large amount of opinions and ideas in a short amount of time

WEAKNESSES

- Information can be less honest. People will be influenced by the group dynamics and will try to present themselves in a positive way
- Danger of leading questions. People may be influenced by the moderator and try to please them by confirming their suggestions
- People are limited to their own personal experiences. Do not expect them to come up with new design ideas but aim to capture their thoughts, feelings and feedback instead
- Strong individuals can dominate the group and influence the other participants
- It is easy to stray from the topic if the workshop not carefully and consistently controlled
- Workshops can be costly and time-consuming to organise. They need to be planned well in advance

HOW

1. Assemble a group of 6-10 people willing to participate in the workshop. Larger groups will be difficult to control while smaller ones will limit the scope. Choose a venue that is of an appropriate size and suitably private.

2. The investigator acts as the moderator facilitating the activities and encouraging discussion. It is essential to have helpers to set up and support activities.

3. Create a structured plan for the workshop and keep to it as much as possible. Timekeeping is critical when working with groups and workshops can be very difficult to manage.

4. Plan for the workshop to last from two hours up to two days depending on the activities and availability of the participants.

5. Start with an ice-breaker that gets everyone involved. This will help to energise and engage participants and help them get to know each other.

6. Aim for a series of short tasks rather than one long one. Use early activities to build up to and prepare the participants.

7. When performing tasks, break the group into teams of 2-4 participants. This makes it easier to control and encourages different opinions to be heard.

8. Get the teams to take ownership of their ideas and get them to present to the other teams. Mild competitiveness between teams can sometimes be beneficial.

9. Stationery such as whiteboards and post-its should be provided. 'Post-it walls' allow everyone to have their say and enables ranking and grouping of ideas. People should not have to bring anything with them.

10. Breaks and refreshments should be provided especially for longer workshops but these need to be strictly controlled in order to maintain momentum.

11. Collect data periodically. Photograph and collect the material that has been generated throughout the workshop and not only at the end.

12. Set aside time immediately afterward to note down key points or ideas before you forget them.

GOES WELL WITH

- Design provocations: props and visual provocations can be useful to inspire the group or as starting points for discussions and activities

- Questionnaires: questionnaires given to the group before a workshop can help you to gather background information on the participants and prime them for the discussion

BEST SUITED TO

- Exploring broad topics from different perspectives and brainstorming new ideas

- Focusing attention on big issues that need detailed discussion

- Providing feedback and challenging existing ideas and designs

- Collecting opinions from a community rather than an individual

HIGH CONTACT
3. EVALUATION

Testing prototypes and design concepts with different user groups for detailed feedback and evaluation. This can be used to validate an idea, iteratively improve it and provide data on how well aspects of the design will perform.

WHEN

Use iteratively throughout the development process but particularly as a design progresses towards the final idea

ISSUES

- Choose users carefully: Make sure you have a wide range of lead users within your target market
- Choose whether to test ideas with people that you have already conducted research with in order to make use of their familiarity with the project, or whether to use new people for a fresh perspective
- Do you test for a couple of hours or ask people to test for longer periods?

STRENGTHS

- Feedback from a user perspective on a full range of design characteristics including aesthetics, function, ergonomics, user-friendliness etc.
- Can test ideas at varying levels of completeness
- Brings fresh opinions to a design that you are by now very familiar with
- Can catch obvious design flaws early on, giving you time to address them
- Ideas tested in 'real-world' scenarios. Lead users will test the idea in unexpected ways adding a robustness to your approach
- Can compare your potential solutions against existing ideas from competitors to benchmark your idea before it goes to market

WEAKNESSES

- Users can be influenced by the appearance and sophistication of the prototype. This may bias the feedback on other aspects of the design
- Feedback from users may influence the design in favour of their own specific needs
- Be careful when basing design decisions on the opinions of a small number of users. You must retain the role of the editor. Not everything that every user says is correct
- Users may lack the experience or training to give useful feedback. Many may just say "It's OK" and not articulate any further
- Testing out of context will provide limited insight while in-depth testing in context can be time consuming to conduct

HOW

1. Start testing as early as possible before too many decisions have been made. This will save you spending a lot of time on solutions that do not work.

2. Plan what you want to test and tailor this to suit the current stage of the design work. An early test may include an 10 minute assessment of simple functionality. Later tests may include in-depth testing over several weeks.

3. Increase the scope of your evaluation as the design progresses. Start by testing the first impressions, and build up to use over a longer period of time.

4. The number of users will vary depending on the scope and nature of the design. Aim to find 8-10 different users.

5. Test with one user at a time whenever possible to get more focused feedback.

6. Try to test alternative solutions. It is often easier to give comparative feedback than to assess a single design.

7. Try to test the idea in context and in a variety of circumstances.

8. Test one time too many rather than one time too few. Your users' knowledge and growing experience of the product is a valuable resource.

9. Document the testing through video and photographs. This is important for analysing and sharing the information with the rest of your team.

GOES WELL WITH

- Interview: ask users to give feedback on prototype features in relation to current products and experiences

- Controlled observation: when introducing a prototype or setting tasks to test functionality, use controlled observation and ask users to verbalise their reactions and thoughts

- Research kits: suitable for lengthier tests carried out in context such as an individual's home. A research kit could be developed to capture feedback whilst the prototype is being used

BEST SUITED TO

- Checking the design throughout the development process across the full range of characteristics from function and ergonomics to materials and finish

- Comparative testing of alternatives to focus on the best solution to take forward

- In-depth testing of an idea before going to market

CASES

This section presents business case studies drawn from across the globe and from different design disciplines. Two types of examples are presented. Short cases highlighting inspirational methodologies and longer cases taking you through the whole approach from research, through development, to launch in the marketplace.

POWER TOOLS
Sandbug and Gofer

FACTS

Client: B&Q (UK hardware store)
Designer: Matthew White,
Royal College of Art Helen Hamlyn Centre

PROBLEM
Home improvement is a very popular activity especially among those of retirement age with more spare time. But power tools, essential to many basic tasks, can be heavy, difficult to operate and more suited to professional builders. This project aimed to develop new products for the B&Q power tools range that included the needs of older users and those with reduced strength.

APPROACH
- Lead users: Older people ranging in age from 60 to 85 with a mix of gender and familiarity with power tools. Women in their twenties.
- Initial methods: Audit of existing tools. Two-minute interview with older shoppers in hardware stores to quickly understand context and issues. Workshop with eight people aged 75-85 to test existing power tools and observe difficulties in set-up and handling.
- Additional methods: It was necessary to see how older people lived with existing power tools on a daily basis. Tools were left for up to two weeks with individuals who were then interviewed about their usage. Some people had never used a power tool and others were very familiar with them. One user was a retired carpenter selected to give expert input.
- Evaluation: Prototypes were tested in focus groups and with people in their homes. Women in their twenties were added to see how younger age groups would react to the designs.

RESULT
Two product concepts were developed and taken to market by B&Q: Gofer, a compact cordless screwdriver; and Sandbug, a handstrap palm sander. Both ideas addressed key ease-of-use factors such as size, weight, form and icons. Gofer has an ergonomic, pebble-shape that fits into the palm of the hand and requires less grip or strength to operate. The electric motor turns on automatically when pressed into the screw and it docks to recharge like a mobile phone. Sandbug can also be more easily held due to its shape and adds a handstrap to make it more secure. The sandpaper is held on by Velcro rather than using complicated fastenings.

The designs were a commercial hit, importantly being marketed as lifestyle products rather than being specifically aimed at older people. Customers from all age groups and genders bought them. In 2005, a national newspaper in the UK included them in a list of desirable designs alongside Apple's iPod.

TELECOMMUNICATIONS

TwoTone Phone

FACTS

Client: BT (UK telecommunications company)
Designers: Matt Harrison and Cian Plumbe, Royal College of Art Helen Hamlyn Centre

PROBLEM

Approximately 14 million people in the UK over the age of 50 are digitally excluded having never used the internet before. This project set out to develop creative new ways to connect older people to the communication benefits of broadband.

APPROACH

- Lead users: Six people aged over 60 who grew up without computers. Represented a mix in terms of age, gender, cultural background, physical proximity to their family, whether living alone or with a partner, and urban or rural location.
- Initial methods: Email questionnaire and formal interviews to establish context. Controlled observation of one user at her computer to quickly understand problems.
- Additional methods: Interviewing older people about broadband yielded few results as it was an unfamiliar subject. As a result, six tester design concepts were created that illustrated easier ways to access or benefit from the internet. These included a piggy bank that displays your bank balance and a simplified keyboard that groups keys alphabetically. Users were interviewed in their homes where these concepts gave a starting point for discussion.
- Evaluation: Ideas were assessed by the users and ranked. This determined the most relevant design for them and provided an evidence-base for taking it forward.

RESULT

The TwoTone Phone is effectively two phones in one unit. The white face acts as a normal, cordless landline phone but the black face is a Voice Over Internet Protocol (VoIP) phone that utilises existing VoIP services to allow calls to be made over a broadband connection. Turning over the phone activates its different modes. The VoIP mode does not have a screen but has six large buttons on which users can write the names of their closest friends and family. The buttons turn orange if the person is online and flash when that person calls, with the added benefit of indicating who is available to chat.

Whilst designed with the older person in mind, the concept is aimed at the mainstream market. Users can connect the phone to their television in order to make video calls and the base unit also acts as a wireless router. For the digitally excluded, it provides a simple way to communicate freely, using previously unexploited broadband services. Several aspects of this design were patented by BT.

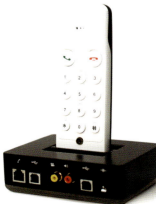

HOMEWARE

Tuva cutlery

FACTS

Client: HardangerBestikk
Designer: Per Finne, Per Finne Industridesign

PROBLEM

Cutlery is used every day but different people hold their cutlery in different ways. Not all cutlery is suitable for people with varying hand sizes or grip strength. The aim was to design attractive, new cutlery that could be suitable for a wider range of people by making it easier to handle.

" I think curiosity about the user is important when you work as a designer"

APPROACH

- Lead users: Children, older people with reduced grip ability and people with physical difficulties as well as adult users without special needs.
- Initial methods: Interviews with different lead users to build up background information in addition to previous obtained user information on cutlery.
- Additional methods: Controlled and natural observation in different contexts looking at how people use their knife, spoon and fork. Study of the placement of the cutlery in the hand and how each individual used their fingers.
- Evaluation: Based on the insights from the interviews and observations, sketch models were prepared and tested with a selection of lead users. This was conducted as one to one interviews between the user and the designer, taking place in the users' homes and at the designer's house.

RESULT

The final concept was hollow-handled cutlery welded together from two parts resulting in a fuller balanced grip without compromising the weight or use of material. The cutlery can be gripped in a number of different ways making it easier for people with reduced mobility and grip strength to use. By following a user-driven approach throughout the design process it was possible to create aesthetic cutlery that is suitable as a wedding gift but equally, can be used by everyone. During the first year Tuva was launched, the manufacturer sold over 100,000 items, 100% over the budgeted sales figure.

SERVICE
Blanke Ark Election System

FACTS

Client: Norwegian Ministry of Local Government and Regional Development
Designers: Øyvind Grønlie from Innovativoli Industridesign, Jan Walter Parr from Kadabra Produktdesign, Line Hagen and Margaretha Andreassen from Blueroom Designstudio

PROBLEM
The current election equipment in Norway has been difficult for voters with common disabilities to access. Ballots were unreachable for wheelchair users and visually impaired people could not vote without asking for assistance in the booth – a violation of the rules of a closed election. This project looked at how the ballot and booth system could be redesigned to make government elections accessible and appealing for everyone.

APPROACH
- Lead users: Visually impaired people, older people, people with reduced physical ability as well as cleaners and election officers who could provide detailed insights into existing problems.
- Initial methods: Phone conversations and face-to-face interviews with lead users provided insights and inspiration that helped to establish design specification.
- Additional methods: Presentation of mock-ups and sketches to lead users to adjust and select initial designs. These were built as full-scale prototypes for testing in situ. At this stage, a reference group consisting of lead users was established to follow the project until completion. They gave feedback on general concept directions as well as design details, taking ideas through several iterations. They gave the green light on the final product specification.
- Evaluation: Questionnaires and focus groups were used to collect feedback and a team of observers followed people on election day to assess the new designs.

RESULT
Blanke Ark can be accessed by voters with different abilities. The graphic profile of all elements is consistent. Black text and symbols are displayed on a white background and the deliberate use of orange attracts greater attention to selected elements. Orange guide tape provides a good contrast against most floors. Booths have two table heights to accommodate standing and sitting voters and are wide enough to accommodate a wheelchair. Labelling for the ballot papers have a suitable font size for low vision users and ballot papers are folded removing the need for 'difficult to access' envelopes. The curtain now has a high contrast orange rod to make it easier to handle. The ballot box, where the ballot paper is posted, is placed at a height that wheelchair users can reach. The opening is high contrast orange and shaped to aid those with unsteady hands or visual impairment.

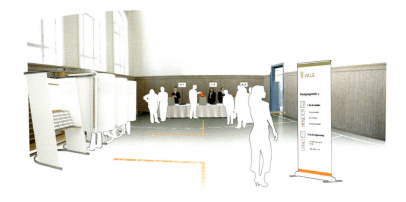

AUTOMOTIVE
Connected Car

NORSK DESIGNRÅD
NORWEGIAN DESIGN COUNCIL

> **FACTS**
>
> **Clients:** TH!NK, Norwegian Design Council, Research Council of Norway (IT Funk)
> **Designer:** Filip Krnja, Royal College of Art Helen Hamlyn Centre

PROBLEM

Car manufacturers face many new challenges such as an increasing number of older drivers, congested cities and carbon pollution. However, the current layout of car cockpits also struggles to integrate new communication devices and increased information flow.
This project, with Norwegian electric car company Think, investigated the potential of the vehicle to become a mobile information interface offering services that go beyond social networking or route planning to enable seamless digital connectivity between the car, home, workplace, family, friends and the city.

APPROACH

- Lead users: 15 people between the ages of 24 and 82. These included people who disliked cars and those who were totally dependent on their vehicles for personal or professional reasons.
- Methods: People were interviewed and observed whilst going about their daily routines. They were asked to respond to a series of images, questions and provocations designed to give insight into their mobility requirements and attitudes to digital connectivity. Many people were interviewed in their vehicles or on the street to get a better sense of context.
- Research results: An interactive persona sheet was developed around each individual, giving a detailed snapshot of their lifestyle and needs. These were a good way to capture the results, communicate them to the clients and develop user insights into rich inspiration for the design briefs.

RESULT

The design ideas support the drivers and passengers of tomorrow - across the spread of ages, functional abilities and personal preferences. A flexible dashboard provides opportunities for customisation: older people can make the dials larger and have higher contrast whilst different 'Apps' such as weather forecast or flight arrival information can be downloaded to the display. Preferences can be carried from car to car on any digital device or key. A digitally connected parked car could switch on to provide street lighting for passers by, act as a wi-fi hotspot, advertise local shops or even point a lost tourist in the right direction. It can also be preheated and defrosted from your home. A digitally connected car on the road might communicate with other vehicles or let people know its location and estimated time of arrival. To reduce visual clutter, the interface adapts to different situations and drivers, displaying information only when required.

TRANSPORT

The subway in Fukuoka City in Japan demonstrates an exemplary approach to Inclusive Design. Over a ten-year period, 16 stations, facilities, signage, rail-yards, ventilation towers and subway car designs were developed and implemented. Research was conducted with a diversity of travellers, all with different needs and demands.

PRIMARY QUESTION
The Nanakuma line that connects downtown Fukuoka with the Southwestern suburbs had limited budget when being built. This resulted in a narrow tunnel cross-section and smaller subway carriages. How could a complex city subway system be designed within this limited space but in a way that was easier and more enjoyable for a wide variety of people to use?

LEAD USERS
In order to ensure that the transport system would be more convenient for everyone to use, many different subway passengers were consulted in the development process. Those who found it difficult to travel around existing public transport were selected as lead users. These were divided into two main groups:
- People with limited mobility: Pregnant women, parents with children, older people, wheelchair users, people with other physical impairments and travellers with heavy loads.
- People with limited ability to access information: Foreign visitors who did not speak Japanese, people with visual or hearing impairments, people with cognitive impairments, older travellers and children.

METHODS
The lead users were brought in for the early stages of the design process during the first year and continually involved throughout the rest of the project. The designers saw their involvement as an essential part of the process and influential in making key decisions. Detailed research was conducted with them at every stage. Different research tools were used as follows:
- Questionnaires: These surveyed a large sample of people and give the designers an early understanding of user needs.
- Controlled observation with Interviews: Lead users were asked to travel through subway systems. Difficulties were observed and logged and individuals were interviewed in situ. Video cameras (see below) were used to document this process.
- Evaluation: Lead users were asked to give feedback as the designs developed.

"I think that the line is the most comfortable subway in the world for people with any kind of disabilities"

Toshimitsu Sadamura, GA-TAP Inc.

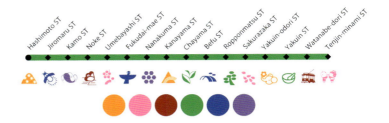

INSIGHTS

This research gave critical insights showing potential areas for improvement. Some selected examples are given below:

Wheelchair users: Were not able to cross over floor height changes. They needed more space to move and change direction. Could not reach buttons for lifts or ticket machines that were placed out of reach.

"Information is placed too high for me to read"

Older people: Could not walk quickly or for long distances. Needed resting points. Could not read small text and did not like confusing information. Needed more time to orientate themselves.

"I need more time when walking"

Pregnant women: Had difficulty moving and perceiving floor height changes or irregularities.

Foreign visitors: Did not understand Japanese behaviour or patterns of movement in public spaces. Information in Japanese typically excluded this group.

DESIGN PROCESS

The design objectives were to create an environment with good mobility and less barriers as well as information that could be easily understood by everyone. A large number of staff worked to solve the different problems on the stations, subways, cars and information systems. Guidelines were formulated for the team to ensure an Inclusive Design approach at all stages.

Considerations in the design process included:
– Design policy
– Concept formulation
– Architecture
– Sign design
– Basic design for a standard station and fleet yard
– Station operations equipment and car design
– Advertising and PR
– Implementation and construction management

FACTS

Client: Fukuoka City Transportation Bureau, Japan
Design and user research: Toshimitsu Sadamura, GA-TAP Inc.
Background: The city subway project in Fukuoka City in Japan started in 1995 and opened in 2005. It is one of the first transportation systems in the world to have a comprehensive Inclusive Design approach

RESULT
The design solutions concentrated on six areas. A few improvements are mentioned under each:

1. **Universal movement lines**
Station layouts allow passengers to move freely through the architecture using the shortest route possible. Entrances and exits always have an elevator or escalator and subway cars equipped for wheelchair users stop by the elevator. The height difference and gap between the platform and subway car are minimal. Getting on and off is safer than other systems.

2. **Universal facilities**
Ticket machines are mounted lower than usual to accommodate wheelchair users as well as standing passengers. They are angled upwards for easier access. The magnetic tip of the white cane carried by visually impaired users automatically calls the elevator and opens the doors via sensors. Accent colours have been added to stair edges to make them more visible.

3. **Universal walkways**
A number of design features make the narrow dimensions of the subway less noticeable and the stations brighter and more comfortable. Large atriums and transparent materials are used to bring natural light underground and provide a feeling of spaciousness.

4. **Visual information**
The colour green is used to identify the Nanakuma line from entrances at street level to ticket machines and restroom walls.

5. **Individual station information**
Each station has its own colour, wall material and unique symbol making it easier for children and non-Japanese speakers to identify. The symbols use animals, plants or everyday objects that are instantly recognisable.

6. **Universal signage**
Children and wheelchair users have a lower eye level than standing travellers so signs are positioned at a height midway between the two. Audible signs direct visually impaired people removing the reliance on difficult-to-recognise Braille.

Overall, this in-depth, people-centred approach helped the designers to innovate in a very cost effective manner and invent creative solutions. The Nanakuma line has attracted worldwide attention and won several awards as an Inclusive Design exemplar. It is in daily use in Fukuoka, Japan.

PACKAGING

Jordan is an international brand working within oral care, painting and cleaning tools. Their focus on customers was not reflected in their packaging design. This project resulted in new insights, increased sales and an improved brand profile.

PRIMARY QUESTIONS
How can we make toothbrush packaging more user-friendly and easier to open for a wider range of people? Can an Inclusive Design approach improve communication, increase shelf presence and strengthen brand value?

LEAD USERS
The lead users had a range of abilities.
- People with arthritis provided feedback on handling and accessing the packaging.
- Low vision users gave advice about shelf presence, information graphics and openability through touch rather than sight.
- Children tested how intuitive designs were as well as dexterity issues. Although not the primary consumer group, they gave key information on how easy the designs were to understand.
- Older people with multiple age related impairments tested a variety of factors.

METHODS
- Controlled observation: Lead users were initially observed visiting supermarkets and shops. This aimed to explore the issues around shelf presence and information graphics on existing packaging.
- Interview: Lead users were interviewed as they tested existing toothbrush packaging and 70 other types of packaging. The process was recorded using video and still camera.
- Workshop: Testing was repeated with lead users, from initial concept to market ready solutions. The process was recorded using video and still camera.

INSIGHTS
Many insights were successfully gathered especially in the areas of openability, prioritising information and brand visibility. Examples of quotes from the users:

"I like larger handles"
80 year old man

"I usually try to open them in the store, if I don't think I can manage, I hang it neatly back in place"
43 year old with arthritis

Above: The previous toothbrush packaging

FACTS

Company: Jordan AS
Design and user research: Kode Design
Packaging Design: Hareide Designmill and E-types
Background: This case study was a pilot project for the Norwegian company Jordan in cooperation with the Innovation for All programme at the Norwegian Design Council

"Inclusive Design gives us a competitive edge and we have succeeded in distinguishing ourselves from our competitors"

Bård Bringsrud-Svensen,
Product Development, Jordan AS

DESIGN PROCESS

Step 1: A criteria tool (see page 41) was developed to make sure that critical factors were addressed throughout.
Step 2: Lead users rated openability and how easy it was to find the point of access. They all gave the old packaging a low rating.
Step 3: Initial research was conducted with lead users using Natural observation, Controlled observation and Interviews. Methods were combined and modified to improve interaction with the lead users.
Step 4: Design concepts were developed according to the experience of the lead users. These were filtered using the list of factors in the criteria tool.
Step 5: The new concepts were tested by the original lead users to ensure that their needs were addressed.
Step 6: An internal workshop was held at Jordan to select and refine solutions.
Step 7: Evaluation with lead users tested the final design before finalising.

CRITERIA TOOL: OPENABILITY

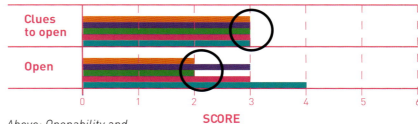

Above: Openability and understanding how to open the packaging presented barriers for all users. The low score on both criteria indicate opportunities for improvement as circled

RESULTS

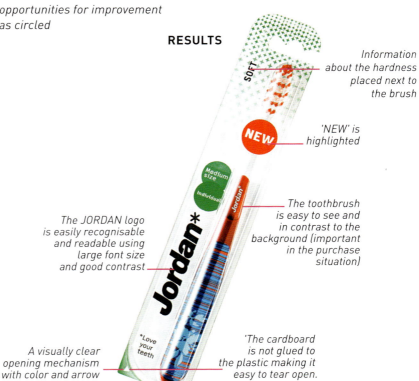

- Information about the hardness placed next to the brush
- 'NEW' is highlighted
- The toothbrush is easy to see and in contrast to the background (important in the purchase situation)
- 'The cardboard is not glued to the plastic making it easy to tear open.
- The JORDAN logo is easily recognisable and readable using large font size and good contrast
- A visually clear opening mechanism with color and arrow

HOUSEHOLD PRODUCTS

OXO is a successful consumer products company whose entire range is based on the principles of Inclusive Design. Since 1990, OXO has grown its flagship Good Grips brand into a collection of over 500 products that have become international bestsellers. A key focus is kitchen utensils.

PRIMARY QUESTION
Inspiration for OXO came after its founder Sam Farber observed his wife's difficulty holding ordinary kitchen tools due to mild arthritis. Farber saw an opportunity to help not only people with reduced dexterity but also to create more comfortable kitchen tools for everyone to use.

> *"We wanted to appeal to the broadest possible market, not just a very specific market of arthritics and the infirm"*
> Sam Farber, Founder, OXO

INSIGHTS
The users in the focus group were all asked what was wrong with existing measuring cups. People answered:

> *"When it's greasy, it becomes slippery"*

> *"If I heat things up it is too hot to touch"*

PROBLEM
Why can't kitchen utensils be designed to be easy to use by people with arthritis?

RESPONSE
Extensive user research and innovative design create comfortable tools for all.

RESULT
Compounded annual growth rate of over 30%.

LEAD USERS
Lead users fell into two categories.
- Expert users. For example if the product is a chef's knife, these would include chefs who use these knives on a daily basis.
- Older people or people with limited dexterity from conditions such as arthritis.

As well as understanding the needs of these two lead user groups, research was also conducted with mainstream users. The aim was to develop solutions that were more comfortable and easier to use without sacrificing efficiency and performance.

METHODS
OXO applies an inclusive approach throughout the design development process and almost every product begins with user observation. The initial idea for the Angled Measuring Cup was proposed by a toy design firm named Bang Zoom. To take this concept through an inclusive development process, Smart Design, a design firm that worked closely with OXO from the beginning, was brought in. They studied existing products to scope the competition and interviewed different lead users to understand the human perspective. In particular, they held workshops and focus groups to explore the physical effects of ageing and observed people with arthritis to identify possible barriers.

These revealed obvious problems but when users were asked to show how they measure liquids a less obvious issue was revealed. Most users would pour, bend down to look at the measurement, pour some out, bend down and look at it again. They had to repeat this process several times. No one in the focus group saw this as a problem. However, the designers focused on this as an opportunity to significantly improve the measuring cup design.

FACTS

Company: OXO
Design: SmartDesign and other independent design consultancies
Background: OXO's mission is to develop innovative consumer products that make everyday living easier for everyone, not just niche markets. Its portfolio consists of 800 products

RESULTS

Research with people formed an integral part of the design process and was central in understanding the unarticulated needs of potential users. Further research into functionality and ergonomics was combined with these user insights to influence the choice of materials, manufacturing techniques, style, weight, look and feel of every product.

In the example of the measuring cup, OXO's innovation was to design a cup that could be read from above instead of the side, removing the need for constant bending over and adjusting. Red text on a white background gives a good colour contrast for most types of liquid.

OXO's Salad Spinner is its most popular product. The salad can be spun by pressing down on the large, black button, removing the need to grip and turn handles as on existing salad spinners. The design is simpler to use and can be operated by wet hands or arthritic hands and takes little strength.

The research carried out by Smart Design for the first set of OXO tools laid the basis for development of the entire Good Grips range and OXO products are among the most widespread utilities of their kind on the international market. The company has effectively used Inclusive Design to develop mainstream commercial successes, that now benefit a wide spectrum of people.

" Our philosophy has not only resulted in user-friendly products for a wider user group; it has also proved to be a profitable business model. We have achieved annual growth of 30 per cent since 1991 and have won more than 100 international design awards"

Alex Lee, President, OXO

Above: The scale can be read from above without the need to bend over

FURNITURE

Norwegian furniture manufacturer Stokke is a worldwide distributor of children's equipment and furniture. TrippTrapp is their award-winning, bestselling children's chair. The idea is an innovation of well-known designer Peter Opsvik and is currently sold in 50 countries.

PRIMARY QUESTION

The idea was born when Opsvik noticed a lack of practical seating solutions as his two year old son outgrew his high chair. He saw the need for a chair that could grow with a child and give them equal presence at an adult-sized table. As nothing existed on the market, he decided to design a solution himself.

LEAD USERS

Primary lead user: Opsvik initially observed his own son and studied his movements at the table to get an idea of the demands that a child would place on the furniture. Other lead users: Children from the neighborhood also acted as lead users showing how the existing solutions did not work for them. Parents played a role as they were key users of the furniture.

METHODS

This example demonstrates the importance of having the right lead user. In this case, Opsvik's son and the other children gave enough insights to inspire an innovative product. Simply observing a few people with a common problem was a powerful way of understanding product need and user aspiration. Natural observation of children was effectively used to see the difficulties with existing, traditional high chairs and define a starting point for design development. This is a suitable technique for conducting research with very young children who might not be able to articulate issues so observation rather than consultation works best. Inclusive Design does not demand large groups of users. Seeing one interesting thing from one user can be enough to get started.

INSIGHTS

Opsvik gained critical insights from observing his users:

- Ergonomics: He saw how children quickly outgrew existing children's chairs and were left sitting on adult chairs with their arms and feet dangling in the air. This was very uncomfortable for them
- Function: High chairs or miniature adult chairs did not fit the hight of a typical adult table. Parents could not sit their children on these chairs and use the table at the same time
- Interaction: High chairs have their own table surface attached which makes it impossible to get close to the family table

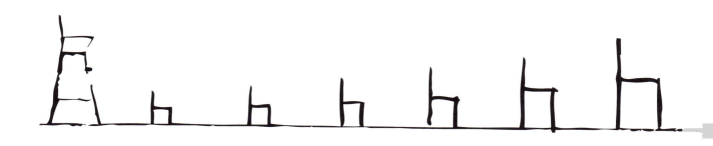

FACTS

Company: Stokke AS
Designer: Peter Opsvik
Background: Opsvik got the idea for Tripp Trapp as he watched his son grow out of his traditional children's chair

DESIGN PROCESS

To solve the problems that he observed, Opsvik designed a chair with both an adjustable seat and footrest. These could be placed at different heights in the frame to fit each user. His objective was that one chair should seat children and adults of different sizes.

Tripp-Trapp has a market share of 90% in Norway, and is sold in 50 countries

RESULTS

The design of the Tripp Trapp chair allows it to be used throughout childhood. It is suitable for children of different ages and positions them so that they can interact and be involved at the same table as everyone else.

Tripp Trapp reflects the designer's vision of creating products for life. The chair is made of wood, ensuring sustainability and longevity.

Tripp Trapps are typically passed down from generation to generation or are circulated on the second-hand market rather than thrown away. Since the chair was launched in 1972 more than seven million have been produced and it has become a significant export product that is distributed worldwide.

"If there's something around us that doesn't work, that annoys us, it can be a good starting point for design. Tripp Trapp started as a solution to a personal challenge"

Peter Opsvik, designer

SERVICE

Scandic

Scandic is one of the Nordic region's leading hotel chains with 151 hotels in ten countries. Their Hotels for All concept implements improvements in their rooms, restaurants and services that will increase accessibility for all guests. During 2010, 150 new rooms will be built for visitors with disabilities.

PRIMARY QUESTION
There are over 50 million people in Europe with some form of disability, but staying at hotels can pose a challenge for many of them. The President and CEO of Scandic, Frank Fiskers, saw accessibility as an important factor to improve desirability and open Scandic hotels to a wider market.

LEAD USERS
Hotel guests with disabilities and members of disability organisations were the lead users. User insights also came from 'expert users' such as Scandic's board of directors and members of the hotel staff by placing them in the situation of lead users with reduced ability.

METHODS
In 2003, the hotel chain engaged Magnus Berglund as its Disability Ambassador. His first course of action was to hire several wheelchairs for Scandic staff to use. Over a time period of three months they were all able to see life from the perspective of a wheelchair user. Although being in a wheelchair is just one of many disabilities, Berglund saw it as an excellent way to get people discussing the issues. This immersive method of research allowed key decision-makers and staff at every level to experience the difficulties firsthand.

Berglund and his team members worked with disabled guests and disability organisations to develop an accessibility standard for their hotels resulting in a 93 point checklist. 77 points are compulsory for every Scandic hotel but all criteria have to be met by new hotels currently being built. The list will be re-examined and extended in 2010.

An important part of accessibility is the quality of service and the attitude of the employees. Every member of the hotel staff is therefore given training to aid them in understanding what they can do to make guests of all abilities more comfortable. This can simply mean placing food in a buffet within sight and reach of everyone or understanding how a hearing loop works.

INSIGHTS
By putting Scandic staff members into a wheelchair, useful insights were discovered firsthand into the needs of people with disabilities.

"Does the mirror need to be so high up?"

"How do I reach the coffee cups at the breakfast buffet?"

Consultation with lead users provided other insights. One person talked about how her mother who has reduced hearing would be woken up by the fire alarm at a hotel. This was the inspiration behind the Scandic vibrating alarm clock that also turns on with the fire alarm.

FACTS

Company: Scandic
User research: Magnus Berglund, Disability Ambassador, Scandic
Background: Scandic began to focus on accessible environments in 2003. In 2009, they became the first hotel chain to place fact sheets about the accessibility of their hotels on their website

RESULTS

Scandic's design process is an ongoing, long-term plan for developing existing hotels, building new rooms and training staff members to have a better understanding of accessibility. Some key features on Scandic's checklist are listed below:

- Height-adjustable bed*
- Telephone on the bedside table along with the remote control
- A space of at least 80 cm around the bed
- Vibrating alarm clock and fire alarm available on request
- Hooks placed at different heights so they can be reached from a wheelchair
- Mirror at a suitable height for wheelchair users as well as standing guests
- Handrail on the inside of doors at a height that can be closed from a wheelchair
- No or low thresholds at doorways
- Single-grip mixer tap or automatic tap*
- Washbasin placed at a minimum height of 78 cm* so a wheelchair will fit under it. The hook, soap and hand towels are also easy to reach
- Toilet paper holder on the armrest of the toilet
- Hearing loop available for meeting rooms
- The doors are at least 80 cm wide, so that guests can get through with a wheelchair, crutches or a walking frame*
- The stage is accessible for wheelchair users*

*Only applies to some hotels.

All these features are not designed to look like "special needs" equipment or add-ons. Better accessibility is something that everyone, including able-bodied guests, can benefit from. Scandic hotels are becoming well placed to attract large numbers of disabled people looking for a better hotel experience.

> "The best proof that we're doing the right thing came from a guest. She told me that when she is staying at Scandic, she is treated just like any other guest and not like a disabled guest"

Magnus Berglund, Disability Ambassador, Scandic

> "A major hotel chain should be accessible even if you've broken a leg, have impaired hearing, use a wheelchair or for other reasons need a little extra consideration"

Frank Fiskers, President and CEO, Scandic

GLOSSARY

Access for All: see Universal Access.
Accessibility: Physical or sensory ability to access buildings, use products and obtain information or services.
Accessible transport: Transport that allows people with disabilities to travel without any obstacles.
Adaptable Design: Design that can be easily adapted to create a barrier-free space, product or environment.
Anthropometry: Study of the measurement of the human body and its physical variations. Anthropometry is an important factor in various disciplines.
Assistive Design: A device that assists a person with disabilities in accomplishing daily tasks. These can include a wheelchair, bath hoist or extendable cutlery to aid with eating.
Assistive technology: Devices that aim to assist or rehabilitate people with severe impairments. Generally not classed as Inclusive Design as the devices might have little application for mainstream markets.
Autism: A spectrum of conditions that includes Aspergers. Autistic individuals have a behavioural condition social communication, interaction and imagination. This can represent in a variety of ways including repetitive behaviour, hypersensitivity to environmental stimuli or adherence to routine.
Barrier-free Design: Modifying buildings or environments so that they can be used by people with disabilities. Automatic doors and ramps are examples of this.
Biomechanics: Study of how mechanical principles apply to living organisms which includes bioengineering and application of engineering principles to and from biological systems. This is an important part of ergonomics and can be valuable in understanding the diversity of human ergonomics.
Co-design: A process whereby end users actively participate in design activities alongside the designer, bringing their ideas into shaping the product, service or environment.
Dementia: Loss of memory primarily due to age that makes it difficult to remember a daily routine. The effect is a serious loss of cognitive ability. More recent memories typically go first.
Design exclusion: Term developed by the i~design research project as a way of understanding who might be excluded by a particular design.
Design for All: See page 9.
Design for Disability: Term used for design considerations focusing on specifically on aids and adaptors for the disabled people.
Design for our Future Selves: Concept developed by DesignAge Programme to encourage young designers to see older people as their own 'future selves'.
Dexterity: Ability to perform manual tasks with skill and ease.
Dignity: Treating people with respect and promoting personal independence.
Disability: Disability can be seen as a result of mismatch between individuals and their social and physical environment. It is important to not define people by their condition. We are all on a spectrum of ability.
Dyslexia: Difficulty in comprehending, writing and reading words and text thought to be due to the result of a neurological defect or difference. It is not regarded as an intellectual disability.
Emphathic research: A form of research based on observation and interview to address the tacit needs and wants of users. Watching without interfering is central to this, adding value to traditional focus group and surveys.
Ergonomic: A product that is designed according to the principles of ergonomics (see below).
Ergonomics: Scientific study that addresses the relation of human being to their environment and the application of anatomical, physiological, psychological,

and engineering knowledge. It intends to maximize efficiency and productivity by reducing operator fatigue and discomfort. *See also Human Factors.*

Ethnography: A branch of social science that primarily conducts research with people. Interviews and observation are traditional tools of ethnography that designers now use in conducting user research.

HTML: HyperText Markup Language used for placing text and graphics on a website.

Human-centred Design: HCD or User Centred Design (UCD) is a term that can apply to any design tailored to users that meet their needs and is intuitive to use. Sometimes used interchangeably with Inclusive Design.

Human Factors: Multidisciplinary scientific study sometimes known as ergonomics devoted to optimising human performance and reducing human error. Human Factors involves the study and development of tools that facilitate the achievement of these goals. *See also Ergonomics.*

Inclusive Design: See page 9.

Investigator: Person conducting research with users.

Method cards: A collection of cards created by design consultancy IDEO representing diverse ways that design teams can understand the people they are designing for. They make a number of different methods accessible and are divided into four categories – Learn, Look, Ask and Try.

Mobility: Ability to moving freely across the city using public or private transport regardless of age or ability. Can also impact an individual's participation in the economic, political and social life of the community.

Number-centred methods: Methods for researching or gathering data that are primarily based on statistics, large samples and percentages.

People-centred Design: A design process in which research with people is central. People are not treated like test subjects but as an integral and equal part of the research process. The term is based on Inclusive Design and sometimes used interchangeably.

Seven principles of Universal Design: Developed by US architect Ron Mace and the Center for Universal Design, North Carolina State University, these principles have formed a benchmark in Universal Design thinking. In summary, they look at safety, comfort, convenience, ease of use, ergonomic fit, suitability, and user value.

Social inclusion: A term that refers to the action being taken against social problems such as unemployment, poor education, ill health, low income, crime, poor housing or poor environment. Inclusive Design has been seen as a tool to promote social inclusion and equality by many governments.

Tactile signs: Signs that have raised letters or markings to be read and interpreted by tracing with fingers over the surfaces. Braille is an example of a tactile language using dots that is primarily aimed at visually impaired people.

Trans-generational Design: Design of residential environments and consumer products that are attractive and accommodating to people across the age spectrum. In general, trans-generational designs accommodate rather than discriminate and sympathise rather than stigmatise older people.

Universal access: The ability to have equal opportunity and access to a service or product regardless of social class, ethnicity, background or ability. Also described as Access for All.

Universal Design: See page 9.

User-centred Design: A term that is sometimes used interchangeably with people-centred design. It describes design processes in which end users influence the design outcome by being involved in all stages of development. It is very often regarded as 'user testing' and is usually brought in at the end of the product development cycle. The term has become synonymous with interface design, usability and more recently in web development with experience design.

User experience: The perceptions and responses of the person that result from the use or anticipated use of a product, system or service. This includes all their emotions, beliefs, preferences, perceptions, physical and psychological responses, behaviours and accomplishments that occur before, during and after use.

User-focused Design: Design with the user in mind. Similar to user-centred design and mostly used within interactive design and web design.

User research: Conducting research people to understand their experiences, in particular their needs and aspirations. A central part of Inclusive Design and people-centred design.

User scenario: A communication tool and narrative describing foreseeable interactions between users (characters) and a particular design. It provides a design rationale, assesses usability factors and gives an overall evaluation. Storyboards are an example of a visual user scenario and a good way of bringing an idea to life.

FURTHER READING AND REFERENCES

Norwegian public sites:

The Agency for Public Management and eGovernment (DIFI)
www.difi.no

The Delta Centre of Directorate of Health and social affairs
/www.helsedirektoratet.no/deltasenteret

The Directorate of Health and Social affairs
www.helsedirektoratet.no

Equality- and Anti-discrimination ombud (LDO)
ldo.no

Governmental Special Education Support
www.statped.no

The IT Funk program of the Research Council of Norway
www.itfunk.org

Ministry of Children, Equality, and Social Inclusion
www.bld.dep.no

The National Centre of Documentation on Disability
doksenter.custompublish.com

The National Council for Senior Citizens
www.seniorporten.no

The Norwegian Association of the Blind and Partially Sighted (NABP)
www.blindeforbundet.no

Norwegian Association of the Deaf (NDF)
www.deafnet.no

Norwegian Association for the Handicapped (NFU)
www.nfunorge.org

Norwegian Cooperation Forum of Disability Organizations (SAFO)
www.safo.no

Norwegian Design Council Innovation for All Programme
www.norskdesign.no/designforall

Norwegian Federation of Organisations of Disabled People (FFO)
www.ffo.no/no

Norwegian Rheumatism Association
www.revmatiker.no

Plan of Action for Universal Design
www.universal-design.environment.no

The SINTEF Group
www.sintef.no

Standards Norway
www.standard.no

Statistics Norway (SSB)
www.ssb.no

International public sites:

Central Intelligence Agency, The World Factbook (CIA)
https://www.cia.gov/library/publications/the-world-factbook

European Blind Union (EBU)
www.euroblind.org

European Commission Eurostat
epp.eurostat.ec.europa.eu

Scandinavian trend institute (Pej)
www.pejgruppen.dk

United Nations (UN)
www.un.org

The World Bank
web.worldbank.org

World Health Organization (WHO)
www.who.int/en

World Institute for Development Economics Research
www.wider.unu.edu

Other links on Inclusive Design:

Adaptor for visually- and occupational disabled
www.adaptor.no

Center of Inclusive Design and Environmental Access (IDeA), University at Buffalo
www.ap.buffalo.edu/idea

Center of Universal Design (CDI) of the Institute of Technology Sligo, Ireland
www.designinnovation.ie

The Center of Universal Design of North Carolina State University
www.design.ncsu.edu/cud

Design for All, Denmark
www.design-for-alle.dk

Design for All, Sweden
www.designforalla.se

Easy Living Home
www.easylivinghome.co.uk

Ergonomidesign
www.ergonomidesign.com

European Design for All e-Accessibility Network (EdeAN)
www.edean.org

The European Institute for Design and Disability (EIDD)
www.designforalleurope.org

Inclusive Design Survey, Cambridge Engineering Design Centre
www.eng.cam.ac.uk/inclusivedesign/dtisurvey

Inclusive Design Toolkit by BT and i~design programme
www-edc.eng.cam.ac.uk/betterdesign

Institute for Design and Disability, Ireland
www.idd.ie

MediaLT
medialt.no

Resources for designers
www.designingwithpeople.org

RNIB Digital Accessibility team
www.tiresias.org

Royal College of Art Helen Hamlyn Centre
www.nhc.rca.ac.uk

UK Design Council
www.designcouncil.org.uk/About-Design/Design-Techniques/Inclusive-design

Universal Accessibility by Architectural Service Department
www.archsd.gov.hk/english/knowledge_sharing/ua/index.html

Reports:

EIAA Mediascope Europe Study (2008).

Ginnerup, Soren, *Achieving full participation through Universal Design* (2009).

Scandinavian trend institute, *Fra barnevogn til kørestol, – Livsfaser og forbrug*. Part 1 and 2, (2007). Louise Byg Kongsholm.

Scandinavian trend institute, *Med det ene ben i graven og det andet i butikken*, - de nye seniorer (2007).

United Nations, *the Millennium Development Report,* (2007).

World Bank Development Indicators (2008).

Literature:

Brenda, L. and Lunenfeld, P. (2003), Design Research: Methods and Perspectives, MIT Press, USA.

Clarkson, P. J., Coleman, R., Keates, S. and Lebbon, C. (2003), Inclusive Design: Design for the Whole Population, Springer, UK.

Cooper, D.R and Schindler, P. S. (1998), Business Research Methods, Irwin/McGraw-Hill, Singapore.

Keates, S. and Clarkson, P. J. (2003), Countering Design Exclusion: An Introduction to Inclusive Design, Springer, UK.

Vavik, T. (ed.) (2009), Inclusive Buildings, Products and Services – Challenges in Universal Design, Tapir Academic Press, Norway.

William Lidwell, Kritina Holden, Jill Butler (2003) Universal Principles of Design, Rockport publishers.

Wolfgang F.E. Preiser and Elaine Ostroff (2001), Universal Design Handbook, McGraw-Hill, USA.

Photo credits and copyrights:

Bland, Barry, Aaron Fotheringham: Page 18
Dennington, Claire: Page 47, 48
Design for Alle Sweden: Page 22
Ergonomidesign: Page 30
Finne, Per: Page 73, 78
Grønli, Espen: Page 8, 34, 35, 36, 37, 50, 61, 63, 69, 82, 83, 84, 85, 96
Harrison, Matthew: Page 66
Istockphoto: Page 20, 21, 25, 26, 27, 37, 56, 57, 58, 59, 60, 61
Kadabra Design: Page 71, 76, 79
Kanter, Beth: Page 18
Krnja, Filip: Page 51, 80,
Lund, Joacim: Page 19
Norwegian Design Council: 2, 7, 36, 37, 47, 48, 50, 61, 63, 69, 70, 86
Opsvik, Peter: Page 88, 89
Oxo: Page 87
Plumbe, Cian: Page 40, 44, 45, 49, 67, 75
Raudberg, Vestbuss: Page 23
RCA Helen Hamlyn Centre: 44, 46, 49, 50, 51, 60, 64, 65, 66, 67, 68, 72, 76, 77, 78, 80
Ruud, Dvegg, Drammen Kommune: Page 23
Sadamura, Toshimitsu, GA-Tap Inc.: Page 81, 82, 83
Scandic Hotels: Page 90, 91
Stokke AS: Page 86, 87
Swix AS: Page 30
Wright, Alison and Armitage Shanks: Page 7

No photo to be reproduced for commercial purposes without permission

Special thanks to:
Blindeforbundets Førerhundsskole
Gn Resound Norge AS
Norges Blindeforbund
Norges Revmatikerforbund

CONTRIBUTORS

This publication is produced by the Norwegian Design Council (NDC) as part of its Innovation for All Programme. NDC commissioned leading organisations and designers within the field of Inclusive Design to develop the content. The NDC has a strategic collaboration with the Royal College of Art Helen Hamlyn Centre, the main contributor for the book. Norwegian consultancy KODE Design has been working closely with the Innovation for All programme for the last five years. Cian Plumbe and Merih Kunur were Research Associates at the RCA Helen Hamlyn Centre. Cian is co-founder of Studiohead.

NORWEGIAN DESIGN COUNCIL

The Norwegian Design Council promotes the use of design as a strategic tool for innovation in order to create greater value for Norwegian trade and industry.

The NDC is a national strategic body for design in Norway mainly funded by the Ministry of Trade and Industry. Its aim is to increase understanding, knowledge and use of design amongst Norwegian enterprises.

NDC initiated the Innovation for All Programme in 2005. This initiative, directed by Programme Leader Onny Eikhaug, aims to demonstrate the potential of an Inclusive Design approach. It enables knowledge transfer by providing business organisations with information and methods to be easily adopted and implemented in everyday practice. The programme works closely with industry, designers, government and education at a national and international level.

Norwegian Design Council:
www.norskdesign.no
Innovation for All Programme:
www.norskdesign.no/designforalle

RCA HELEN HAMLYN CENTRE

The Royal College of Art Helen Hamlyn Centre provides a focus for people-centred design and innovation. It has gained global recognition for its work in Inclusive Design.

Its multi-disciplinary team of designers, engineers, architects, anthropologists and communication experts undertake practical research and projects with industry to advance an approach to design that is socially inclusive. To date, the Centre's Research Associate programme, now lead by Deputy Director Rama Gheerawo, has completed over 100 projects with 75 organisations from industry, government and the voluntary sector. Many ideas have gone on to positively affect business thinking.

www.hhc.rca.ac.uk

KODE DESIGN

KODE Design is an Oslo-based design consultancy specialising in user-centred innovation. For the last 10 years KODE Design has delivered successful products and services to companies such as HÅG, Tomra, Q-Free, Jordan, Tine and Nera. It has earned numerous international awards and has worked with the NDC to develop Inclusive Design thinking and methodologies through projects with industry.

www.kodedesign.no

STUDIOHEAD

Studiohead is a design and innovation consultancy based in London. Partners Cian Plumbe and Matthew Harrison believe in a user-research orientated approach to design, developed during their experience at the RCA Helen Hamlyn Centre. The studio has a diverse portfolio of projects ranging from fashion products to surgical equipment.

www.studiohead.com

Editor-in-chief: **Onny Eikhaug**, Norwegian Design Council (NDC)

Editor: **Rama Gheerawo**, RCA Helen Hamlyn Centre (HHC)

Contributing authors:
Onny Eikhaug (NDC), **Rama Gheerawo** (HHC), **Cian Plumbe** (Studiohead), **Marianne Støren Berg** (KODE Design), **Merih Kunur** (HHC)

Project Co-writer and Assistant:
Victoria Høisæther (NDC)

Onny Eikhaug   Rama Gheerawo   Cian Plumbe

Marianne Støren Berg   Merih Kunur   Victoria Høisæther